GOIN' BACK T

THE JOY OF LIFE, FISHING AND ROCK 'N' ROLL

Brian Halvorsen

Published by McNidder & Grace
21 Bridge Street
Carmarthen SA31 3JS
Wales, United Kingdom

www.mcnidderandgrace.com

First published by McNidder & Grace 2023

A Catalogue record for this Work is available from the British Library.

ISBN: 9780857162465
Ebook: 9780857162472

Cover design by Tabitha Palmer, Wales
Designed by JS Typesetting Ltd, Porthcawl, Wales

To my beautiful wife and soulmate Lyn who both inspired and assisted me to create this book. Thank you.

SLIDING DOORS

'I think I'm goin' back
To the things I learned so well in my youth
I think I'm returning to
All those days when I was young enough to know the truth'

'Goin' Back' by Gerry Goffin and Carole King

Do you wonder what your life would have been if decisions made by your parents, when you were young, had been different?

In my case, when I was just seven, my parents, younger sister Lynne, and I moved from the now fashionable and expensive Bethnal Green, to pastures new. That part of London's East End, in the 1950s and early '60s, was the opposite of expensive, trendy and the place to be. It was slowly recovering from the destruction of the Blitz, and there was decrepit housing and bombed buildings yet to be cleared. The vast open bomb site that was virtually next to our rented flat made for a great exploration and play area for my small gang of friends and me. Although we would unearth personal objects that had been buried since the war, no human remains, or unexploded bombs came to light on our playtime watch.

Virtually all the housing would have been classified as slum dwellings, with poor sanitation and no hot running water. Many had outside toilets and central heating was unknown. Taking a bath would entail us sitting in a big tin tub warmed by water from a large kettle. I would use the same water as my parents. The only place to take our weekly bath, especially in the winter, was close to an open fire in the lounge. Aged five, I was hospitalised, and my tonsils were removed as a solution to my chronic ill health, which in reflection, was most likely a consequence of my damp, mouldy, toxic home conditions and the ever-present air pollution. The Great Smog of London 1952 caused the deaths of up to 12,000 people from respiratory diseases, mostly in the East End.

Nonetheless, many East Enders loved their local environment, which in turn created a spirit of family and community. I, however, look back at the anti-Semitism and violence that abounded at the time. The Krays were accepted as part of the social fabric and were more respected by the locals than the police. Even when walking the streets, either on my own, or with my small group of friends, I would have to appear and act tough. As a 6-year-old, I learned either to run away, or to fight other gangs of kids often older than me. At school, or returning home, or even returning from Saturday morning pictures, I was often set upon, kicked and punched. I would give as much as I received – an attitude that earned me local respect, but for all the wrong reasons. Today I can understand the circumstances that would lead to youngsters getting involved in gangs. I believe that the environment of many deprived areas, especially of inner cities, can be, and often are, the breeding grounds for criminality and violent anti-social behaviour. If I hadn't moved out of London, would a life of crime have been an option for myself?

My uncle, Len, was not only one of life's characters, but also one of the most famous and flamboyant of the market traders in the East End's Club Row Market. He would draw in huge crowds to watch his carefully choreographed show. Fine china dinner sets would be tossed in the air with a great display of panache and showmanship. Although he was "Givin' 'em away for nuffin" – well, the cup and saucers – he would make a small fortune on the complete dinner set. Most of the profits would then be lost betting on the Dogs. In Southampton, Uncle Len even shared the Mayor's parking spot outside the Dog Track.

As a teenager I worked for Uncle Len for a week leading up to Christmas. I soon realised that being a market trader was a very hard existence, especially in the winter. During his shows Uncle Len would make me the stooge by announcing that despite attending a grammar school, I was next to useless and slow on the uptake. He would describe me, his nephew, with Yiddish words such as *klutz,*

lutz, putz, schmuck and *meshugener*. He paid me well – in cash, of course. I worked for only one week just before Christmas, returning home with a stinking cold. I then spent the next 48 hours in bed recuperating, once was enough for me.

My father had been taking me through the 'lanes' near to the famous Petticoat Lane market to see Len's show for years, ever since I was four. On a Sunday morning the crowds were so tightly packed that we couldn't move forward. My father's solution was to take me off his shoulders and instruct me to kick anyone in our path. People would turn and look down in annoyance, to which my father would innocently shrug his shoulders and also look down at me, in fake annoyance.

Due to the ubiquitous pollution, I was often unwell with breathing problems. Besides having my lungs clinically collapsed in hospital, I remember waking up with a sore throat aged five, after having a tonsillectomy. A classic case of treat the symptoms rather than the cause.

My other abiding memory of Bethnal Green was its lampposts. Walking with my mother, totally absorbed in conversation, I turned to headbutt an ornamental lamppost. The swelling above my left eyebrow became so large that it had to be incised to reduce it. When I mentioned to my mother that there are scars over both of my eyes, she smiled and said that a few weeks later I managed the exact same collision. Different lamppost, different eye.

At the age of six, I found myself sitting in a large black chair with a man in a white coat, coming towards me holding a black rubber mask, which I remember was the source of an unpleasant acrid rubbery smell. Instead of forcing the mask over my face, he stood in front of me and asked if I knew about astronauts, and the lack of breathable air in space. Being a young clever dick, I nodded in agreement and asked him what the mask was for.

'This,' he said, 'is for delivering a new type of air to the men in space so they can breathe; and I am wondering if you would like to try it.' I nodded and immediately grabbed the mask from the anaesthetist and started gulping in the 'air'.

The next thing that I am aware of, after having had four permanent molar teeth extracted, was blood pouring out of my mouth and my mum asking if I was alright – which I was. When I look back, how lucky I was to be treated by a holistic practitioner; my first encounter with surgical dentistry was without trauma. Many of my past patient's dental phobias have stemmed from upsetting experiences in the dental chair as a child.

The move from the grey dirty grime of the East End of London to Bracknell, a new town in rural leafy Berkshire, was a milestone in my life. Our newly built new three-bedroom terraced house was part of a Green Field development to relocate people like my family away from the London slums to planned new housing estates – in our case to Easthampstead. Initially, living in our rented council house was like being part of a building site, surrounded by partially completed houses, roads, and a part-built shopping precinct. The continued and constant construction and expansion of the adjacent housing estates, along with being surrounded by open countryside, made for the best playground I could have wished for. I swapped playing in the decrepit and destroyed bombed sites of the East End of London for green open countryside and woods where we could build our own camps with materials 'borrowed' from the builders. And what woods and countryside there were to be explored and enjoyed within a short walk from our house! I loved my new environment, and the freedom to turn it into my magical playground.

> 'But every day can be
> a magic carpet ride.'
> 'Goin' Back'

With my new-found estate chums, many who are still friends today, we tramped the woods and heathland at any opportunity. We loved all the excitement of climbing trees, finding bird's nests, identifying bird species, spotting rabbits, hares, foxes, deer, stoats and weasels and the great delights of playing with snakes, frogs, tadpoles and newts. Every outing was an adventure and a voyage of discovery. The only limited factors were attending school, appalling weather and being home for meals.

Most of my friends and I tried the Scouts but found the formality and lack of spontaneity boring – and there was too much conformism in our opinion. Instead, we created our own fun activities.

We became quite good at making camps and cooking outdoors. Lighting a fire with straw, twigs and branches, we would place large potatoes in the hot ashes and roast a hock of bacon, bought for a few pennies. Our method of cooking the joint was to suspend it over the flames in an open-ended tin can. Baked beans would complete the feast. Besides the feeling of being young chefs, the food by our standards at the time, was delicious. My life in the wilds of leafy Berkshire was as close to adventure paradise that I could ever have imagined.

Playing in the bomb sites of London might have been reckless, and fraught with numerous dangers. Playing in the countryside turned out to be equally hazardous. On one occasion, our campfire quickly spread to the overhanging tree. Within a few minutes the blaze was out of control. Rather than risking being discovered as the culprits, we decided that the best thing to do was to sneak off. On the way home we were reassured by hearing the sirens of the fire engines; the rest of the wood was saved.

The only requirement our parents would demand was punctuality for meals and to come home with all shoes, wellies and clothes intact. By today's standards we would be regarded as feral. While raiding an orchard containing a variety of fruit trees and bushes, and enjoying eating strawberries, gooseberries and damsons, we were chased by the Green Man – the equivalent of today's community police officer. In making our escape, Graham, one of our occasional friends, ran into a single horizontal plant frame wire. Once we had made our escape, Graham who had been covering his mouth with his hands, decided to show us the resulting trauma. The sight of his lower lip flopping independently in two parts horrified us and we suggested that a visit to the hospital would be appropriate. Although there was hardly any blood, the lip had been completely severed, involving the whole lip tissue through to his chin. After treatment and although the scar was virtually imperceptible, Graham declined future invites to join our outings.

During that summer holiday, we decided to build a large tree camp in one of the massive old oak trees that grew in a field on the edge of our housing estate. The climb was difficult, and the platform of the tree house was at least 20 feet above ground. Much of the 'borrowed' material was winched up to me as chief designer and builder.

On one occasion, a heavy club hammer slipped out of my hand and decided to fall to the ground. Its descent was interrupted by James's head, despite me shouting 'Fore!'. Unfortunately the hammer did as its name suggested; clubbed him. Building work was temporarily cancelled while we carted him home. Thankfully, we did not think the blow had any long-term effects; he went on to be CEO of several major high-tech companies and is an excellent golfer!

All around the estate, the builders were digging ditches for laying pipes, new footings, etc. These 'trenches' were the ideal environment for war games. We would gather as many of the local estate kids as possible to form opposing armies, taking cover in the trenches. When battle began, large stones and bricks were lobbed at each other, mimicking hand grenades. Although crude shields were used for protection, the bombardment would continue until one side admitted defeat due to the number of injured troops. As far as I know, not a single combatant was hospitalised.

Similar games and regular forays into the wilds of the Berkshire countryside, were only interrupted by attending school. My first educational establishment was a Church of England associated school called St Michael's. It was a short walk from my home and tiny by today's standards, with a total of about sixty kids. The school immediately created a friendly and caring atmosphere. Our form teacher was a kindly lady, a little unconventional by today's standards. On one occasion, I was absorbed in evaluating the theory that if you can grab a snail by its horns (actually retractable eyes) and throw it over your shoulder, the snail will turn into a pot of gold, and I completely forgot about the time. Eventually my teacher came outside and asked me in a kindly way if I would be re-joining her class indoors. On explaining what I was doing, she changed the subject of the lesson and sent the rest of the class to collect and study slugs and snails instead. No snails were mistreated during the class's formal investigation of these invertebrates.

The Easter when I was eight, I was given £5 by the same teacher to leave class, walk a half-mile to the local shops to purchase enough Mini Easter eggs for all my class – and twenty Player's Navy Cut cigarettes for herself! Not only could I buy the cigarettes without question, but she suggested that if there was any change, I could keep it. Those were the days.

Attending St Michael's offered the opportunity to make new friends, though this was not always obvious at the time. I was recently reminded about my first encounter with Frank. Frank became a lifelong best mate after I flattened him with a carefully aimed blow to his head during a discussion at playtime.

A year later, most of my class was moved to a newly built junior school. It was larger, with more spacious and modern classrooms and extensive playing fields. I quickly settled and made lots of new friends. On one occasion, a friend and I were summoned to the headmaster for making too much noise playing machine guns with the stilts that we had been using for PE. Admittedly we should have been in class and the whole school could hear the racket we were making, but the punishment that was meted out to both of us was a tad brutal by today's standards, a single very forceful and painful smack on the back of our bare legs. My indelible memory was of the red mark on my leg. Not only could I make out the exact outline of his hand, but I was convinced I could also see the detail of his hand's joints and lifelines. When I arrived home and wearing short trousers, there was no hiding the hand mark. Once noticed by my parents, without an ounce of sympathy, their only comment was: 'Whatever you got up to, we're sure you deserved it. Serves you right.'

1960

I was nine at the start of the decade, and unaware of the significance of changes that were happening to the world at large. The introduction of the oral contraceptive pill, the shooting down of a U-2 spy plane by the Soviet Union, the continued testing and expansion of nuclear weapons, a massive Ban the Bomb rally in London, and the USA's increasing involvement in Vietnam would have massive implications for the future of the world.

Not that I was paying much attention. I may have been top of the school in general knowledge competitions and had an intelligent interest in current affairs, but my comprehension of the significance of the events was minimal. There were far more important things to do, such as living within my boyish imagination and spending time playing games with friends.

Living on a new council estate had many advantages, such as a ready-made group of friends of a similar age group, both boys and girls. Although the opposite sex was beginning to hold an attraction and a fascination for me, most of my spare time was spent with my male friends, playing games and roaming the local woods and countryside. Collecting wild bird's eggs created a purpose to our forays. Back then, amassing egg collections was regarded as commonplace. If our mission was to collect a particular species of a bird's egg, we would walk comparatively vast distances, such as a 6-mile walk to Virginia Water to obtain the egg of a Great Crested Grebe.

The severe winter of 1962/63 killed millions of our wild bird population. In March 1963 while walking through deep snow, which hadn't melted in three months, we found hundreds of dead birds of all species. Appalled by the carnage, we all made the decision to stop collecting wild birds' eggs. I sold my collection for the royal sum of £5, the equivalent of £100 in today's money. By contrast, when I started a landscape gardening job in 1961, my hourly rate was 2 shillings (10p) per hour.

Besides my love of walking and exploring the countryside, I remember 1960 for playing Cowboys and Indians and war games with my estate friends. It was only fifteen years since the end of the Second World War and there had been many films made in the intervening years: *The Dam Busters*, *The Bridge on the River Kwai*, *The Cockleshell Heroes*, to name a few. For us kids, there weren't any shades of grey. One of our detailed discussions revolved around being captured by the Japs and imagining the pain of bamboo shoots growing slowly through our bodies after we had been captured and pegged out in the sun. At home, many hours were spent setting up battles with our Dinky Toys and die-cast soldiers.

During that summer, our parents allowed us to camp overnight in a large overgrown field next to the estate. We didn't tell them that there was an abundance of adders and grass snakes. In our own way, we did a risk assessment: 'A bite from an adder will kill you within 2–3 hours; therefore, plenty of time to rush home and call the ambulance.' Our flimsy sleeping bags and tents were uncomfortable and primitive, but the immense enjoyment came from cooking a ham hock over an open fire, large, blackened potatoes baked in the ashes with lashings of baked beans – heavenly. It may have been the beans, but most of the following morning was occupied with an extraordinary and prolonged farting competition. The winner was the idiot who could remain in the small, stench-laden tent the longest.

Although I spent most of my waking hours completely absorbed with either school or my friends, time spent at home, especially during the winter and periods of poor weather, led to an increasing dependence on television and radio. The news media was starting to invade my waking hours.

I had a serious inquiring mind, curious about history and current events. Newspapers, radio and TV were the sources, and I was keen to absorb as much as I could, especially historical and documentary programmes. Any documentary involving battles of the world wars was compulsory viewing – but only if my parents allowed me to stay up past my bedtime.

(Then, or course, there were great cartoons such as *Popeye*, *Yogi Bear*, *The Flintstones* and *Captain Pugwash*.)

Television and radio were not only increasing my worldly awareness, including the differing genres of music, but changing the perspective of a whole generation.

In my own mind, the doubts were building. I came to realise that there were things happening in the outside world. Not everything that I was told or read, especially in the media, was the entire truth. Discussions about current affairs at school often led to more questions than answers.

My childlike innocence and subjective self-imagination were slowly being eroded by a new reality.

An event that aroused my intense interest, as the child of a Jewish mother, was the capture of the Nazi war criminal Adolf Eichmann. Kidnapped by Mossad and smuggled out of Buenos Aires, Argentina, he was to face trial in Israel, for his role in helping to organise the Holocaust. Eichmann was labelled 'chief executioner' – and I couldn't understand why there was so much condemnation of Israel's actions by many countries, especially the United States and Argentina. Why were countries like Argentina, supported by the United States, openly shielding mass murderers? My global perspective of fair and righteous societies was being rapidly eroded.

> 'I think I'm returning to
> Those days when I was young enough to know the truth.'
> 'Goin' Back'

My sex education, however, took a giant step forward when *Lady Chatterley's Lover* by D.H. Lawrence was released, following a highly controversial court case. A copy was purloined from one of our parents and did the rounds on our estate. I managed to 'critically review' it from cover to cover. I loved the euphemistic descriptions such as 'his John Thomas'.

By this time, I had completely grown out of Saturday morning pictures, thinking it uncool for kids of my age, many of my classic big hero films were showing at the local cinema. Here were very clearly defined examples of 'good versus bad', 'heroes and villains' and the correcting of various forms of social injustices. Some of my favourites were:

Ben Hur – starring Charlton Heston.

Spartacus – starring Kirk Douglas.

The Magnificent Seven – starring Yul Brynner, Steve McQueen, Charles Bronson and James Coburn.

The Alamo – starring John Wayne.

My age meant that neither my friends nor I could see adult films. My friends and I were told that during the showing of these films, the back row of the cinema was filled with couples snogging and getting up to no good. I did not know what that meant at the time.

My family had owned a black and white television set for a few years, and in 1960 we watched the opening episodes of *Coronation Street*. Far more exciting for me was the western series like *Rawhide* starring Clint Eastwood playing Rowdy Yates. Clint Walker starring in the series *Cheyenne Bodie*, was also a hero of mine.

* * *

I was increasingly becoming exposed to music of all genres, mainly via television and radio. Much of it came from America. Although there wasn't an official chart in 1960, retail sales of sheet music and vinyl records would supply a fairly accurate guide to what was popular. The music played on television and radio was a mixed bag, with lots of music from the movies. Some of my fun and most liked songs, for all sorts of reasons in 1960, were an eclectic mix:

Sam Cooke – 'Chain Gang' (Toilets)

Frankie Laine – 'Rawhide' (sore bum) and other 'Cowboy and Indian' pop music such as, Johnny Preston's 'Running Bear' (We thought Bare) and The Shadows' 'Apache'.

Cliff Richard and The Shadows – 'Lucille', 'Please Don't Tease'; he did create quite a good rocker image at the start of his long career.

Eddie Cochran – 'Three Steps to Heaven'

Tommy Steele – 'Little White Bull'

Lonnie Donegal – 'My Old Man's A Dustman' [Daft song, but we all sang along.]

Peter Sellers and Sophia Loren – 'Goodness Gracious Me'

The King Brothers – 'Standing on the Corner'. Now would be regarded as suspicious undesirable behaviour.

Roy Orbison – 'Only the Lonely' – Great song, great voice. The words had a resonance with me.

Rocky Valance – 'Tell Laura I Love Her'

Elvis Presley – 'It's Now or Never'

'Dam Busters March' from the war film *The Dam Busters*. – Out came our paper and combs and with outstretched arms, making out we were Lancaster Bombers.

Johnny Kidd and the Pirates – 'Shakin' All Over' – this was for me was one of the first great rock and roll pop songs.

Although the playing of 'pop' music on the radiogram and television was random and mixed with other music genres, there were some all-time greats that both my parents and I appreciated.

Buddy Holly – Although killed in 1959, his songs were played throughout the '60s and his music inspired virtually all the great rockers. The Rolling Stones had their first Top 10 single with a cover of Holly's 'Not Fade Away'.

The Beatles chose their name as a kind of homage to The Crickets, and Paul McCartney has since purchased Buddy Holly's publishing rights.

Some of the songs I enjoyed in 1960 and beyond are:

Buddy Holly – 'That'll Be the Day', 'Peggy Sue', Every Day', 'Oh Boy', 'Think It Over', True Love Ways' 'Rave On', Raining in My Heart', 'Everyday', 'Words of Love'.

Drifters – 'Save the Last Dance for Me'.

Neil Sedaka – 'Oh Carol'. – Rumoured to have been written for Carole King.

Brian Hyland. – 'Itsy Bitsy Teenie Weenie Yellow Polka Dot Bikini' (A silly one.)

Elvis at that time, was not on my musical radar. I wasn't a fan of the slicked back, greasy look adopted by so many Rockers, including the young Cliff Richard.

Although pop music was often in the background and blasted out in places such as circuses, fairs and fairgrounds, my immediate focus was my local friends and the adventures that we could dream up.

One of our more ambitious ventures occurred in the early summer of that year. Stephen was a fearless, gifted tree climber who like me, had a collection of wild bird's eggs. Having studied the Isle of Purbeck in detail at school, we decided to travel by public transport to Swanage, Dorset, in search of gulls' eggs. If successful, the impressively large speckled brown egg would be the pride of our collections.

Approaching Old Harry Rocks, the path was very close to the sheer, 200ft-high chalk cliffs and were terrifyingly dangerous. At regular intervals we would crawl to the cliff edge and peer over to look for a nest. I was comfortable with heights, but looking down at the rocks below made me distinctly nervous. Eventually Steven spotted two Herring gull's eggs on a narrow ledge about 6ft from the cliff top. As there wasn't anything to hold onto except a few tufts of grass, I pleaded with him to give up the venture. Next thing I knew, Stephen had sidled along the ledge with one of the eggs in his hand. He then asked me to take the egg from him so that he could collect the other one. This meant me going over the edge. Saying that I did this with a certain amount of trepidation would be an understatement. My only 'security' was a large clump of grass. We did both made it home, and the large speckled brown egg was the pride of my collection. However, when I look back now, my only thought is: *foolhardy!*

Having survived, I took the 11+ exams. To sit in the school assembly room, in complete silence, writing answers to questions from a test paper that thousands of other kids my age were also answering, was a new experience. I ploughed my way through the maths and English questions. I loved reading adventure books such as the Allan Quartermain series by H. Rider Haggard. Being inspired by these stories and not having a clue about what else I could write about, my exam essay was an adventure, not in Africa, but a journey up the Amazon.

Naively, throughout the whole of the exam process, I was oblivious to the importance and significance that these exams would have on my future. Pass, and I would be heading for a grammar school. Fail, and it would be the local secondary modern.

I was lucky enough to pass. In those days there wasn't any coaching by my school to boost their statistics. I was considered a bright kid, representing the school in general knowledge quizzes and being near the top of the class when we had our daily mental arithmetic tests. I was genuinely ambivalent about my academic future and far more interested in my school friends and teammates. Unfortunately, most of my local playmates did not pass, leaving just a few friends to accompany me to a new school. That was next year, so school and my life continued as normal.

I started to become interested in the variety of school sports and was very proud to be part of the winning team in the district school's soccer final, which at the time for me was a huge achievement. My other claim to fame was throwing a cricket ball the full length of a football pitch, thereby setting a school record that lasted for many years.

Although I loved the outdoor life, there were days when severe weather forced me to stay in and to find things to occupy my time. I found salvation in making and playing with Airfix model aeroplanes. Over a period of time, I had a reasonable collection of warplanes from the Second World War. Each one came with a very detailed description of their construction, performance and function. Among my collection were the Spitfire, Hurricane, Mosquito, Lancaster bomber, Me 262, and my very favourite, a seaplane called a Short Sunderland.

In late October, the availability of fireworks, especially bangers, meant that all our available funds were invested in the most explosive devices we could afford. I managed to obtain a dozen extra-large bangers, labelled dangerous. When my family were out of the house, I invited a few trusted friends to bring their planes around to play 'shoot down and crash'. From the upstairs window, we would launch a plane with lighted banger(s) in the fuselage. The skill came from timing the fuse so that the aeroplane would explode in the very brief time that it was flying. I launched the massive Short Sunderland, loaded with four bangers, and the spectacle of it blowing up in mid-air was our talking point for weeks to come.

Watching my favourite film stars, one of my burning issues of that time was my hair. Normally, I was told by my parents to get my haircut and given the correct money, job done. At the barber's, there was a choice between 'short back and sides' or shorter 'short back and sides'. Seeing the stylish haircuts of the male film and pop stars, my mates and I were questioning the bog-standard cuts that we all were receiving. At my next visit to the hair salon, otherwise known as the barbers, I requested to keep the sides longer and have the hair cut straight across at the back, a style called a Boston. I was fed up with my hair at the back of my head which tapered into the nape of my neck. My friends regularly pointed out that this looked like a 'duck's arse'. The outcome? To quote the hair stylist: 'Get out, you little git, and don't come back.'

I was allowed to attend my father's Christmas works party. Besides the food and a few furtive smiles from an attractive girl about my age, the 'Do' was a complete waste of time. Then there was an announcement: The next dance is 'The Twist' by Chubby Checker. It was an amazing sight to see the adults perform all sorts of contorted movements and trying to appear trendy. I tried to explain to my parents that the dance technique was about imagining drying your back with a large towel and rotating both feet in the opposite direction. Rather than give a demonstration, I sat on a hard wooden chair on the edge of the dance floor, sipping my first alcoholic drink – Babycham – and feeling like a nearly grown-up. Attending the party was one of the co-owners of the tailoring factory, a famous ventriloquist called Peter Brough. As a cool 10-year-old, I didn't find it amusing being photographed sitting on his knee talking to his famous dummy, Archie Andrews. When I showed my friends the photograph, the immediate comment was, 'Who's the dummy?'

The year ended with John F Kennedy being elected as the next president of the USA. None of us could have conceived what lay ahead.

1961

After receiving the news in March that I had passed the 11+ exams, my year at junior school continued normally. We really didn't give much thought or discussion to the changes that were ahead of us. I would be starting my new school in September, which seemed an age away. I continued playing with my friends from the estate and school with not a care in the world. As our gang enlarged, including girls, our games became more diverse to include marbles, jacks, hopscotch, arm wrestling and mini games of football and rounders. I regard this time as one of the most idyllic episodes of my childhood. There was a period in spring, after school, when a friend of mine and I would meet our girlfriends in the beech woods close to our school and compete for how long we could maintain a kiss without drawing breath.

In those romantic woods, when not distracted by kissing, my attention was drawn to bird spotting and noting holes in the beech and oak trees where jackdaws or owls may be nesting.

Many evenings were spent indoors playing all forms of games, including Monopoly. After a while we were hooked on card games such as poker and brag for money. The stakes were in pennies and thruppennies, but on a winning streak, I could afford a new Dinky Toy. Besides being an enjoyable time filler, it also gave me some extra pocket money; well, on most occasions.

The mad axeman

A few miles away from my home in Easthampstead was the infamous prison for 'the criminally and mentally insane' – Broadmoor

Hospital. In the case of an escape, the local population would be warned by a siren. Every Monday morning at 10 a.m. the siren could be heard for miles around and would sound off for two minutes as a practice drill. All surrounding schools had to keep pupils in class until the all-clear sounded. On one occasion, the wail of the siren continued. As it was a Thursday, we quickly realised that this wasn't a rehearsal; this was the real thing. The schoolteachers remained calm and made sure that either our parents collected us, or we walked home in groups. Although this was the only subject of conversation on the estate, most people weren't overly concerned.

An axe murderer had escaped and was thought to be hiding in the local woods. That evening, the situation was reported on national television with a warning that members of the public should stay home and not enter the cordoned-off area or approach the criminal under any circumstances. Because we lived so close to the prison, police vans drove slowly around our estate asking all residents to go into lockdown, as the fugitive was known to be especially violent, having chopped up his victims with an axe and being regarded as out of control even by the notorious Kray Brothers.

The escapee, labelled The Mad Axeman, was regarded as extremely dangerous and vast resources were being put in place, including tracker dogs, helicopters, hundreds of soldiers and police with firearms to recapture him.

Four of us thought it would be a great idea to go hunting the madman. It was a pleasant surprise that our parents allowed us to go out and play, with the only proviso that we did not to stray too far from the estate and to be back for supper. Having nodded our agreement, we armed ourselves with sticks and set forth.

We had watched the news on television, and the Axeman was described as 'having a limp and wearing an old brown coat'. No mention of an axe! Our plan was to walk to a particular sector of the forest that we thought would make a good hiding place for a fugitive. The spot was well known to us and coincided with the authority's prime search area.

It's very surprising that four urchins carrying long sticks were not stopped from entering the restricted woodland. We had been walking for only a few minutes when we reached a clearing in the forest, and only 50 yards in front of us, a limping man wearing a brown raincoat appeared. Having seen us, he scurried off into the undergrowth carrying a long stick.

Just at that moment a search helicopter circled overhead and landed in the clearing after frantic waving on our part. Out jumped assorted police officers, some with weapons. We pointed to where the madman was heading, and off they went. In the helicopter there was a press photographer who took a statement from us, then lined us up for a photograph and took our names and addresses.

thorne, combined in a spectacular manhunt.

GREAT STRENGTH

Police, in great strength, descended on Broadmoor, setting up their operational headquarters in the social hall across from the high red brick wall surrounding the Institution buildings.

There were patrol cars, wireless cars, vans with police dogs inside, and police service vehicles, large and small.

Later in the morning lorry and coach loads of servicemen from the R.E.M.E. Ferranti Ltd., was loaned free of charge to the police to help them in their search. It was piloted by Major R. Smith, the firm's chief helicopter test pilot.

For most of the day the search was concentrated around woods at the Caesars Camp area, between Crowthorne and Bracknell.

First positive evidence that Upcher was still so close to Broadmoor was given by 48-year-old Mr. Leslie Purver, a Forestry Commission warrener, living at the Forestry House, Crowthorne.

Mr. Purver described how shot gun, which he kept for squirrels, but he did not want to get it out.

Within minutes of Mr. Purver's alarm police in patrol cars and on motor cycles as well as tracker dogs had raced to the scene.

As the hunt progressed the centre of the search switched backwards and forwards, as reports of the escaper being spotted came in — from all directions.

Late on Monday afternoon one report placed Upcher as having been seen crossing the main road into Bracknell.

Left to right: Frank Pipe, David Little, David Page, Brian Halvosen.

Frank is on the far left – note the tie!

Frank, for some obscure reason, was not let out to play that day without wearing a tie. Perhaps his mum had a premonition of his impending fame!

It was a big mistake to give our real names and let our photographs be taken. Instead of being regarded as mini heroes, we received a massive telling-off from both our school and parents.

By the way, they did catch the Mad Axeman not that many miles from where we had spotted him. Without his axe, but still in possession of a long pole!

Norway

Little known to me, my parents had organised a five-week holiday to my father's homeland of Norway. I would be staying with my grandparents. Besides never having flown in an aeroplane, I would also be making the flight on my own! This was going to be quite an experience.

I was led to believe by my parents that the trip was a reward for passing the 11+. However, I did have a faint suspicion that they just wanted to get shot of me for the summer holidays.

I entered the aeroplane, alone, curious and extremely excited. Apparently, we were to be one of the first flights to land at the newly opened Oslo Airport. The aeroplane was powered by propellers, and my lasting memory was of the cabin crew being truly caring and kind to me. I had a paper label on my pullover bearing the words 'unaccompanied minor'.

I was greeted at Oslo airport by three of my Norwegian uncles – Frank, Herman and Halvar (I know, Halvar Halvorsen!). None could speak any English, but they smiled a lot. The journey from Oslo to Nalum is over 80 miles and although this was the main coastal road labelled the E 18, it was like a poorly maintained A road. With the wealth that followed from the discovery of oil, most of Norway's roads have now been vastly improved. The E 18 is now a superb motorway.

After several hours of little communication, uncle Halvar stopped his classic VW Beetle in a lay-by on an isolated stretch of the highway. All three uncles turned to me and exclaimed 'Piss?' As a sheltered 10-year-old, I thought this was a bit strong. However, we all climbed out of the car and pissed on its wheels. Later I found out that my uncles had been told that this was a polite way of asking, 'Would you like a wee-wee?'.

Where the fishing started

Nalum is a small village on the coast of Norway's Oslo fjord. In the nearby mini fjord, there are some small but lovely sandy beaches. These are rare along this part of the coastline and consequently are extremely popular as a summer holiday destination for Norwegians, especially from Oslo. Today the whole area is a destination for holidaymakers with vast areas around the fjord allocated for caravaners and campers. When I first arrived in Nalum in 1961, there was a general store and not much else.

Opposite the store was a traditional Scandinavian house, where I was to stay for most of my trip. It was the home of my grandparents, who had lived in Nalum all their lives, bringing up eleven children, including my late father, Bjarne. Although very little English was spoken, I was warmly welcomed and very quickly felt at home.

Me by Uncle Halvar's Volkswagon

I have always loved exploring the great outdoors, and all the associated wildlife. The countryside around Nalum did not disappoint me, with the added bonus of the sea less than a mile along a track. Most days I would set out on my own, walking past summer houses (*hyttes*) which were interspersed between rocky outcrops and woods. Some of the wooden summer houses belonged to my uncles and aunts. Later into my stay, I helped my grandfather nail the felt roofing onto uncle Sverre's *hytte*, which is still there today. My primary destination, however, was a part of the fjord where many small fishing boats were moored. This mini harbour was called the *brygge* and it now became my go-to place.

On the way along the rough track, I would come across bugs, poisonous snakes, and furry animals that I have never seen in England. The bird life was also different; hooded crows, Arctic terns and many songbirds that were rare or that I had never come across beforehand. Another bonus was finding and eating wild blueberries and strawberries. Even today, there is nothing to beat the taste of the small, perfectly ripe, wild wood strawberry.

Bypassing uncle Halvar's *hytte*, I would approach the fjord by a sheltered mini natural shallow bay, where many of my uncles kept their small wooden fishing boats, and where the 'harbour' was surrounded by smooth rocks running sheer into the sea. Having made it to the sea, I would spend endless hours clambering over the rocks, exploring the rock pools, and making hideouts in the concrete bunkers created during the Nazi occupation of Norway in the Second World War. For a boy, having complete freedom to roam and explore this particular part of the Norwegian coast and countryside, was like being the proverbial pig in clover. My only mandate was to be back for meals, which were both enormous and delicious.

It was a lovely warm and bright morning, and I was following my regular route around the Nalum fjord, when I saw a beautiful lady emerging from the sea. It was just like the beach scene from *Dr No* as Ursula Andress emerges from the sea in front of Sean Connery (not that the film had been released yet). The only difference was that I was standing stupefied and gulping at a lady who approached me stark naked! She stopped to pick up her towel – and in perfect English, asked me if I had lost a penknife, which I was indeed looking for at the time. When I nodded, this goddess asked me to escort her back to her *hytte*. I will let you imagine what was going through my 10-year-old mind as we walked and chatted. She was a very nice Dutch lady on holiday with her boyfriend. After a cup of coffee and a pleasant chat, she gave me my penknife back, I thanked her, and we said our goodbyes.

After a couple of weeks of my stay, Uncle Frank mentioned something about *fiske*. In Norwegian, 'fishing' can mean one of two things – fishing for fish or looking for girls. I imagined that he was referring to the former. Later that day, Uncle Frank and I set off on my normal route to the sea but instead of stopping by the boats we headed to where the fjord joined the open sea. We didn't have any equipment such as fishing rods or nets, so I assumed we were just going for a walk.

When we arrived at a shallow beach area, Uncle Frank gestured for me to collect some sea snails and mussels and produced a small plastic bag from his trouser pocket. It did not take long to fill it with foraged wildlife. We then walked across a large expanse of smooth rocks and sea grass meadows and continued on our walk. On the way, Uncle Frank was constantly looking at the ground, and eventually found a block of cork and a suitable shaped stone.

I was still none the wiser.

After about a half-mile walk across open coastal fields, we clambered along the granite cliff face, to reach a ledge which was about 10 ft above the deep blue-green sea. Uncle Frank produced from his trouser pocket a coil of monofilament fishing line and a hook about size 4 or 6. With my prized penknife he shaped the cork and tied it to the fishing line as a float, followed by the stone as a weight, and lastly the hook. We had a fishing rig! I was clueless about what was to come.

Uncle Frank found a large smooth stone and used it to smash a few live snail shells. After threading them onto the hook as bait, he cast the rig underarm, about 15 yards into the sea.

We watched the float bobbing up and down.

It suddenly disappeared under the surface and did not come back up. Uncle Frank handed me the ball of line and shouted something like 'Uppa'. I started to retrieve the tackle but found there was strong resistance to my efforts. Uncle Frank shouted, 'Bra fiske (Good fish)'. After about a 10-minute tug of war, the fish was against the rock face, and it took both of us to carefully lift it onto our ledge.

My heart was thumping with a mixture of excitement, pride and physical exertion. Lying before us was a 5–6 lb Norway haddock – predominately silver/orange with spiky dorsal fins. At the time, the weight and species of this superb specimen was irrelevant. Uncle Frank indicated that the fish was bony and would be great for making a fish soup. I was ecstatic – hooked.

The world of fishing had arrived for me, and none too soon. If I had previously thought my lifestyle was good, it had now reached a new dimension, it had become superb.

More than sixty years into the future and I cannot ignore any river, pond, lake, or marine environment. They all still have a fascination for me. What lies beneath the surface and how can I catch it?

Fjord side, not only did I want to rebait the hook, I also wanted to hand-cast it out again. This was accomplished reasonably well, and within a few minutes the cork float disappeared. After another good fight a beautiful 2 lb wrasse was flapping on the rocks in front of us – this time entirely by my own efforts. We fished for another hour, catching two more wrasse, and four sizeable haddock. The haddock we ate that evening, the wrasse was used in my uncles' crab pots. My grandmother was impressed by the freshly caught haddock, and they tasted heavenly. Uncle Halvar indicated that the spot where we fished was potentially dangerous, and the family were surprised that Uncle Frank had taken me there. I was told that under no account should I go there on my own.

Besides the feeling of accomplishment and excitement, there stirred a deep sense of awakening. Perhaps this is linked to our primordial origins? Anyway, I loved every moment of my very first fishing trip and every day thereafter my first waking thought was for another fishing adventure.

Two days later, after my persistent nagging, Uncle Frank agreed to take me back to the same spot. The weather and sea conditions were perfect. The fishing was great, and we caught wrasse, haddock and a few small cod. This time, Uncle Frank let me do all the fishing while he sat on the ledge smoking his pipe.

All was going well until I hooked my finger. The hook had penetrated the fleshy part of my forefinger, beyond the depth of the barb. For the non-fishers, a barb is designed to prevent a hook from pulling out in the opposite direction from where it entered. Not much pain, but Uncle Frank was scratching his head as to how to get the hook out. Eventually, I was told to squeeze my hooked finger while he carefully ripped the hook out. Once the hook with a chunk of my flesh had separated from my finger, we decided that a fresh snail would be a better bait than my finger. Thankfully by squeezing hard, I felt little pain and there wasn't much bleeding. The finger was wrapped tightly in a bit of cloth, and I continued fishing. Uncle Frank explained that I should not say anything to the rest of the family, as that would lead to a ban on any future fishing trips.

A few days later, I was shipped to Horton, a large town on the Oslo fjord, where my Uncle Svere lived with his wife Aslaug and their two children, my cousins Bjorn and Rigmor. Although Bjorn was a couple of years older than me, it didn't alter the fun we had together, including fishing from the pier with a short fishing rod.

Fifty-five years after my visit, Bjorn asked me if I remembered teaching him to play poker. I asked him why. He said, 'By playing by your rules, I couldn't understand why you kept winning money and I kept losing it.'

Fishing on the pier with cousins Bjorn and Rigmor

During my stay with Bjorn and his family, he suggested a trip to the cinema. The film was *A-Haunting We will Go*, starring Laurel and Hardy. It was in English with Norwegian sub-titles and proved to be one of the funniest films that I have ever seen. However, an amusing dynamic quickly developed. I appeared to be the only English person in the theatre and laughed a split second before the audience, who were relying on the subtitles; soon they realised that if I howled with laughter something hilarious was coming!

When I returned to Nalum, the weather was perfect: sunshine and calm seas. One evening my uncles had planned a boat fishing trip in the fjord. To say I was excited would be an understatement. Three boats set out from the *brigge*. I was in Uncle Halvar's boat armed with hand lines, and for bait, cooked prawns or live mussels. We anchored where the fjord joined the open sea. The sea was about 130–165 feet deep, and a deep grey blue. The technique was to drop the 4-ounce weight to hit the seabed and then lift the line, so the bait was just above the bottom. Almost at once there was a tugging on my line, and I did not need any prompting to haul the fish aboard. 'Vitting (whiting),' Halvar exclaimed with genuine excitement. I was soon to discover why.

After a few hours and with a boat load of whiting and large mackerel, we pulled up the anchor and headed for shore. A crowd had gathered by the shore of my uncles, aunts and cousins. A large open fire was already blazing to barbecue our catch. The flavour of freshly caught whiting was incredible. My Norwegian relatives eat all sorts of sea fish as a staple but were raving about the sweet taste of these fresh caught whiting – an incredibly happy ending to a great day.

There were a few more fishing trips, from the rocks as well as the boat but soon my time in Norway would be coming to an end. I had arrived in Norway as a tall 8½ stone weakling. Five weeks later, after spending most of my time walking and climbing over rocks, enjoying the clean, unpolluted fresh sea air, and eating huge amounts of fresh fish and new potatoes, I arrived back in England as a 10 stone fit, strong athletic youngster.

The low cloud formation that greeted my return to Bracknell appeared to symbolise the passing of another phase of my life. And now my immediate mission was to find out the local angling venues and opportunities.

Autumn 1961

Back in England, my thoughts were mainly on all aspects of fishing and talking to my local friends about my adventures in Norway. Although it was time to prepare for the start of a new school and secondary education, my conscious thoughts were in denial of any changes.

Ranelagh

Founded in 1709 by Earl Ranelagh, the school was now a highly regarded Church of England Grammar School. Its setting and appearance created an impression of a private school.

In the '60s, Ranelagh was and still is regarded as a top-grade grammar school. I quickly realised that it was a combination of good fortune and luck that I had gained a placement there. Although being a Church of England assisted school, it was also open to non-fee-paying kids like me. It was also the only co-ed grammar school for many miles around – another stroke of luck. Besides the building looking grand, set in its own grounds, it was run educationally on similar lines to a private school. It was the lifelong ambition of our headmaster to have a sporting fixture with either or both Eton and Harrow schools. It never happened during my time at the school.

My trousers

The few weeks into Michaelmas term, and the change from junior to the senior school protocols became a very different experience. Ranelagh had a strict uniform code. This entailed not only buying the uniform but also the sports kit(s) from an expensive stockist in Bracknell. My mother was not very happy, mainly on financial grounds, but there weren't any alternative options. However, for whatever reason, she decided that my trousers would be sourced elsewhere. As my father worked for a clothing manufacturer of high-class suits, my new grey school trousers were the correct shade, but differed in both texture of material and style. The recommended school trousers were flannel, shapeless and baggy. Mine were smooth, fine weave, fitted, drainpipe – but the correct colour.

I didn't receive any adverse comments from my teachers but unexpectedly created a host of admirers and positive comments especially among the senior school. This had implications both positive and negative. I was the first to be singled out for the new boy's induction. In my case this meant having to spend an entire lunch hour with one of the fifth-form bullies walking me around in a tight headlock. He also played tight head prop for the Under 16 school rugby, and I was asked many times if I wanted to give up. Having endured my trial without complaint, and thanks to my trendy trousers, I was now exempt from any further ordeals, whether beatings or having my head repeatedly flushed in the toilet.

Despite the induction ceremony, I quickly settled into the new school environment. Academically, my previous status as top dog was shattered. Many of my classmates dominated subjects such as maths and the sciences. Languages such as Latin and French were completely foreign to me. However, when it came to school sports, due to my size, strength and speed, I was soon to be selected for the Under 13s' school rugby team. I loved playing with the older boys. During my time at the school, I captained my year group and played regularly for Berkshire at rugby, athletics and basketball. Even so, it was fishing that was to be my passion and priority – at least until involvement with the opposite sex became all important. Until then, all aspects of angling in lakes and rivers dominated my thoughts and leisure time activities.

After school activities

When I arrived back from Norway, my primary intention was to discover places to fish and use fishing tackle suitable for my locale. In conversation with my local estate friend Frank, I described the amazing fishing adventures that I had in Norway. Typically, Frank retorted, 'Me and my dad go fishing to the best places in England and catch whoppers.' Although I knew Frank was – and still is – prone to exaggeration, here was a friend of my age who knew a lot more about fishing than I did. We quickly discovered a local fishing tackle shop, where the owner Eddy, a miserable sod, would grudgingly be a mine of information on all aspects of local fishing venues, tackle and bait, etc. My education in coarse fishing was beginning at a pace, only to be interrupted by school, homework and Saturday rugby matches.

Frank and I started our fishing at Binfield brick pit. Binnie, a mature deep clay-bottomed lake, was sited next to an active industrial site making red clay bricks. Due to a lack of funds, my fishing tackle was primitive but adequate for a total beginner. Fishing at the margins of the lake, we were delighted to catch small perch with worms and pester the serious anglers for advice on how to catch the more challenging fish such as roach, crucian carp and tench. It did not help our cause that when we were bored, we would begin a clay fight. Two or three of us would take up positions on opposite sides of the lake, about 80 –100 yards apart. With the aid of a short stick, we would fire potato-size balls of soft clay with great accuracy at each other. Great fun, but not for the irate anglers trying to get some peace and quiet in order to catch fish. The other by-product of our lakeside battles were our long-suffering parents, who had to wash our clothes and tend to our bruises.

Once school had started, opportunities to visit Binnie became dependent on weather, homework and Saturday rugby matches. As I kept asking for money to help fund my new angling activities, my father sorted me out some manual labouring jobs at weekends, which had the effect of reducing my time fishing. The other limiting factor was the availability of a suitable bait. There's nothing worse than trying to catch fish without bait, but maggots were too expensive. The only alternative was earthworms.

At that time worms were to be our number one bait. After much research and discussion, Frank and I decided to create our own wormery – a bucket or wooden box filled with soil and compost. Used tea bags and tea leaves combined with compost made great worm food. My father was pleasantly surprised when I offered to dig up the flower borders. I called this weeding.

The worms that I collected from the flower borders were small to medium (1–4 inches), which we nicknamed Williams. To collect lobworms (5–8 inches long) we had to wait until after dark, especially after a rainy day. We would search the lawns of our garden or the grassed areas of the housing estate. Armed with a torch and a bait box we would slowly and softly creep across the grass (worms are extremely sensitive to vibration) in search of the elusive lobworm.

At night, large worms come to the surface to feed and mate. They normally do not entirely leave their holes. So, on approaching these randy worms, the technique is to grab the body and gently but firmly tease them out of their holes without breaking their bodies. Watch a blackbird pulling a worm from the lawn and you will see what I mean. We would call our large worms Sir Williams. A worm that exceeded 8 inches would have the honour of being a King William. On the hook, we wondered if a King would either eat or frighten the fish we were trying to catch. A few years later my largest roach, weighing in at 2 lb 1 oz was captured by a King when fishing in the Thames when the water was chocolate brown and in full flood.

Collecting worms, acquiring the appropriate ground-bait and hook baits, visiting the tackle shop, sorting the fishing gear, making sandwiches and a flask of tea were all part of the magical world of preparing for an angling trip. Even now, 60 years on, I have to wait for my fishing buddy Bill to make some sandwiches and a flask of soup before setting off. It is all part of a tradition for us grown-up mature fishermen, feeling and re-enacting the protocols that created the excitement and atmosphere of our past.

During one of my visits to the tackle shop, I spotted a beautiful 13 ft alloy fishing rod. Love at first sight. Price £4. Eddy promised not to sell the rod and gave me 6 months to save for it. My cash flow was one shilling per week pocket money. I needed cash ASAP.

Christmas was coming, so with my mates we organised a carefully planned two weeks of carol singing. We 'worked' the local housing estates with their high-density housing. The romantic picture of carol singers gathered under a porch with the whole family standing by the front door listening with dewy eyes and full of Christmas romance was not how we perceived our commercial model.

Where there was a terrace of houses, we would spread out to stand in front of the doors, often individually. I would orchestrate the opening line, such as 'O come all ye faithful'. Our angelic voices would then ring out in unison. If I say so myself, we collectively had rather good voices. People, on opening their doors, expecting a choir, were often surprised to see a single carol singer. However, most households, on opening their doors, filled with the Christmas spirit and more importantly money in hand, would still hand over the cash. This was carol singing on an industrial scale. Even today I still remember all the words to popular carols. We thoroughly enjoyed the warming atmosphere and generosity of people on their doorsteps and this, together with a substantial income, made our Christmas merry.

It was not long before I was looking for the first opportunity to try out my new dream fishing rod.

For me this was a time of angling discoveries and excitement on many levels. I discovered that Jack Hargreaves presented a brilliant television series called *Gone Fishing*. He captured the holistic nature of being in the countryside, observing the environment, as well as demonstrating angling techniques that I had yet to learn and enjoy. I loved the theme song that accompanied the shows, 'Out of Town', with the words: 'Say what you will, the countryside is still, the only place that I can settle down.'

Sentiments that have always stayed with me.

World awareness

Together with being encouraged to read and research topics associated with my secondary school education, I started to read the *Daily Mirror*. The race to send a man into space would make regular headlines. The first man was the Soviet Yuri Gagarin, followed by the American Alan Shepard. The Cold War aggro between the Soviet Union and America was starting to ratchet up with the debacle of the Bay of Pigs Invasion, a failed attempt to land in Cuba and overthrow the government of Fidel Castro. Spy planes being shot down, a large number of US troops being sent to South Vietnam, and the Soviet Union exploding the largest ever Hydrogen bomb 58 megaton, called Tsar Bomba, all began to add to my general angst. I had started to have concerns that global peace and harmony was looking decidedly uncertain.

The good news as part of the daily read from the *Daily Mirror*, was the inclusion of cartoons such as *Andy Capp*, *The Perishers* and *Garth*. Television cartoons also provided us with many hours of entertainment with shows such as *The Flintstones* and *Deputy Dawg*. My friends and I couldn't stop watching the cartoon series of *Tom and Jerry*, which we found hilarious. Because there was no way of repeating the programs, we made sure that we wouldn't miss an episode.

After watching TV shows such as *The Avengers* and *Danger Man*, my first twinges of materialism and envy came when seeing dashing, well-dressed heroes driving around accompanied by attractive women in the newly launched convertible E-Type Jaguar. I couldn't wait to grow up.

* * *

Compared with today, teenagers in 1961 had limited access to pop music. We relied on TV and radio. There were a few television shows like *Juke Box Jury*, with host David Jacobs, *Pick of the Pops* with Alan Freeman and *Saturday Club* with Brian Mathew. Before he passed away in 2017, I was one of Brian Mathew's S.O.B.s, Sad Old Bastards, who every Saturday morning at 8 a.m. turned on my bedside radio to listen to *Sounds of the Sixties*. With his soft but authoritative presentation Brian always seemed to be a lovely chap and was a mine of information about '60s music.

Having an affordable record player, being able to visit a record/ music shop, and the ability to buy a record single or long player changed the lives of many, including my friend Frank and by association, myself. For the first time in human history, the ability to play your favourite song/ piece of music, in the privacy of your home ad infinitum until the grooves on the vinyl wore out, was open to the working-class masses.

The number of record purchases became the numerical source of the popularity of songs and artists, when compiling the pop charts. As a 10-year-old the new music would become one of my passions. For portable music, the transistor radio – or wireless as it was known – was a must-have. As soon as I could afford one, it was an essential, especially accompanying me on all my future fishing trips. How lucky can anyone be, fishing in idyllic surroundings and being able to listen to some of the best music that was ever made?

In the early '60s, many of the great standard songs had an amazing shelf 'life' in the hit parade, often reappearing months and sometimes years after their initial popularity.

In no particular order, this is my eclectic mixture of 1961:

Chubby Checker – 'Let's Twist Again' – The only dance that I could manage.

Ben E King – 'Stand by Me', and 'Spanish Harlem'

Helen Shapiro – 'Walking back to Happiness'. She topped the charts at 14 years old.

Dave Brubeck – 'Take 5'

Roy Orbison – 'Running Scare' and 'Crying' – I still love both songs.

The Ramrods – 'Riders in the Sky'

John Leyton – 'Johnny Remember Me'

Edith Piaf – '*Non, je ne regrette rien*'

Frankie Vaughn – 'Tower of Strength'

Andy Stuart – 'A Scottish Soldier'

The Regents – 'Barbara Ann' [Covered later by the Beach Boys]

The Drifters – 'Save the Last Dance for Me'

Bobby Vee – 'Rubber Ball'

The Everly Brothers – 'Walk Right Back / Ebony Eyes'

Jorgen Ingman – 'Apache' [Covered by The Shadows]

The Shirelles – 'Dedicated to the One I love'… [Later – Mamas and the Papas]

Ferrante and Teicher – 'Theme from Exodus'. Watched the film, so the Jewish side resonated with me.

The Marvettes – 'Please Mr Postman'. [Later – Beatles]

Del Shannon – 'Runaway'

Kenny Ball – 'Midnight in Moscow' – at a point in time when 'we' regarded Russia as romantic.

Although I wasn't a great fan of Cliff Richard, *The Young Ones* was a film that I saw at the cinema and enjoyed. The title song was good and had relevant lyrics for me.

Many of the above became hits in later years for other acts. In my view, 1961 was not a great year, but it was the precursor to the amazing and fantastic music that the rest of the '60s would be known for.

1962

A momentous year in world history. I was absorbed by sports, games, fishing and an increasing interest in the opposite sex and pop music, but even so I noticed the Cuban missile crisis (16 October – 20 November), which challenged my belief in a safe and secure world.

Cuban missile crisis

Until this possible apocalyptic situation, reading and watching news reports of wars and threats of conflict in other parts of the world was to me like being an observer, detached from the likelihood of any personal consequences.

I read Nevil Shute's *On the Beach*, which describes the consequences of a third world war.

> *'It's not the end of the world at all,' he said 'it's only the end of us. The world will go on just the same, only we shan't be in it. I dare say it will get along all right without us.'*

With this in mind, public broadcasts showing the effects of a nuclear explosion and advice or 'look away from the blast, stay indoors and shelter under a kitchen table' didn't exactly fill me or most people with confidence.

In response to the deployment of American Jupiter ballistic missiles in the Balkans and Italy aimed at Russia, together with the failed Bay of Pigs invasion of Cuba, the Soviets agreed to supply similar types of nuclear missiles to the Island of Cuba. The logic was both tit for tat and to deter a future invasion.

After many months of negotiations, the situation became critical in October and the world was on tenterhooks for over a month.

As the tensions between the Soviet Union and the United States mounted, the media started estimating lives lost if a limited nuclear war was to break out – 100 million Russians; 100 million Americans. Even at my age, I realised that a nuclear war would lead to Armageddon – no more fishing for me.

Except for the Cuban Missile Crisis, most of the events of 1962 had little impact on me at the time. Nelson Mandela was jailed in South Africa, Marilyn Monroe died, there was another deadly London Smog, Brian Epstein became the manager of the Beatles, Golden Wonder launched the first flavoured crisps (cheese and onion) – and I barely noticed.

In 1962, television consisted of two main channels, BBC and ITV. My friends and I would often discuss and critique programs especially if there were new releases. These included:

> *Z-Cars*, which was a bit more realistic than *Dixon of Dock Green* and had a tune that we could play with our paper and combs.
>
> *Steptoe and Son.*
>
> *University Challenge*. Originally with Bamber Gascoigne; it's still going.
>
> *The Saint*. With Roger Moore. Lucky so and so! Always getting the girls.
>
> *That Was the Week That Was*. First real satire programme, most of the humour was over my head.

There were also many great films released during 1962 that did interest me, including the first in the series of James Bond movies – *Dr No*. Who then didn't want to be 007? *West Side Story*, *El Cid*, *Lawrence of Arabia* were other blockbuster films that I would see and enjoy, when or if they came around to our local cinema.

* * *

Attending a grammar school was proving academically challenging. Latin and French verbs, pronouns, etc were double Dutch to me. Homework was proving to be a nightmare. I had to try and knuckle down!

At the end of the first year, our two classes were divided into A and B. I scraped into the A-stream.

Out of body experience

During a rainy lunchtime, a group of my school friends and I were experimenting with the effects of the Valsalva manoeuvre. Having discussed the technique during a biology lesson and been told by our teacher that it could be potentially dangerous, we were of course prompted into action. When it was my turn, I duly sat on a chair, took a deep breath, held it, pinched my nose and closed my mouth as my chest was squeezed by a classmate from behind. I immediately lost consciousness and collapsed.

My next image was looking down at my slumped body from the rafters of the room with my classmates standing around 'me' looking and sounding concerned. Both vision and sound were clear and precise; 'I' was an observer of my own body. There wasn't any sense of concern or emotion, and any realisation of time disappeared. In fact, it was a matter of a few seconds before I regained consciousness.

I did not have any perception of re-entering my body. My friends told me that I was in an unconscious state for less than a minute and not long enough for them to be worried that they may have killed me.

I must add that this was a dangerous experiment and should never be attempted unless under medical supervision.

Although I never mentioned the event to anyone, until many years later, it created a profound sense of confusion and anxiety. The immediate aftermath was a feeling of not being part of the world. Questions arose in my mind: *Had I lost or damaged part of my brain? Was I now permanently detached from the 'real world'? Was I still 'normal'?*

For the next few days, I was going through my everyday routines as a spectator. After a few weeks, my overall feeling of 'living in' my life experiences slowly returned, but my analytical and scientific mind could not comprehend what had happened.

Since them, unexplainable profound events have occurred to me, which have altered my perception and understanding of the 'conscious universe'. The event in that school classroom was shocking at the time, but it has added to my sincere belief that there is a consciousness existing beyond life as we know it.

> 'Let everyone debate the true reality
> I'd rather see the world the way it used to be
> A little bit of freedom's all we lack
> So catch me if you can I'm goin' back'

1962 was a time to improve, indulge and develop skills in all aspects of my sport and leisure time. During the early months the weather dictated my outdoor activities. Rugby and hockey were both new, exciting and fun. The school's indoor sports curriculum of gymnastics, circuit training and basketball added to my inner ambition to be an all-rounder.

Being a novice angler, most of my initial fishing experience was at Binnie Brick pit, and during the cold spells catching fish in a lake was almost impossible. But the weather improved and with the discovery of some other exciting ponds around Bracknell, not to mention improved technique and better fishing gear, I expanded my catches from small perch to small roach, small tench and even some elusive crucian carp. The coarse fishing season ended on 14 March and started again on 16 June. Unlike today, the close season applied to lakes, ponds and canals as well as rivers, whereas now only rivers have a closed season to angling. Whenever the urge became irresistible, we ignored the rules and fished illegally. Many of the senior anglers also seemed to be relaxed about fishing the lakes during the close season.

Although playing with my mates and sport occupied much of my leisure time during the 'closed season', we did enjoy exploring the countryside around the estate, looking for all sorts of wildlife, new birds' nests and potentially new fishing venues. On some of our walks, we would come across a parked car, its suspension creaking, with all the windows closed and steamed up. A few of my older friends would sarcastically say: 'I wonder what they're up to', then bang on the bonnet and we would all run away. I did have an idea, albeit it a bit sketchy! My parents appeared to have forgotten or avoided to tell me about the birds and the bees beforehand, and as time passed, assumed that I knew it all anyway. This assumption was only partially true.

As the day of 16 June approached, our levels of anticipation grew. The long summer days meant we could fish very early until very late, and sometimes fish all night. Night fishing was the perfect environment for enjoying all the elements of camping, cooking, long discussions and the anticipation of catching a monster of the deep. Our first all-night session was at Binnie Brickyard and was more like a camping trip with some fishing thrown in as an extra. Great fun, but all the commotion meant that there were very few fish biting. When the dawn broke and most of the happy campers were fast asleep, we did catch some small perch and roach.

First lesson of coarse fishing: You will not catch many good fish if there is too much noise and thumping around on the bank.

That summer our fishing trips were confined to in and around Bracknell. This was partly due to the increasing amount of fishing gear that we had to cart around with us. Besides my fishing rod and nets, I carried a fishing box, which had a double function: to carry and store equipment and to be used as a seat. Although not a gifted carpenter, I had built my first tackle box with loving care. It lasted for all my trips during the '60s and was to become one of the few sentimental possessions that I kept well beyond its active service. As our method of transport was either walking or a single geared bicycle, we had a limited range of fishing venues. Despite these limitations, time was irrelevant, so life could not have been simpler or freer and easier.

One of our early fishing lessons was to make sure we had enough bait. On several occasions when the fish were biting, our main concern was that we would run out of bait and/or food. We often used the contents of our sandwiches as fish bait. In those early days preparation wasn't our strongest asset. After one of our comparatively long exploration treks, a major discovery of that summer was to stumble across a small pond where we were amazed to spot a shoal of small tench. With the water being clear and deep close to the edge, we could see fish swimming in and out of the weed beds. After catching a couple of tench upwards of half a pound, the pond became our favourite go to venue. I was smitten by the strength and beauty of these fish, and even today the tench is my favourite still water species.

Bushnell's boatyard

In late September and completely out of the blue, a friend of my father asked me if I would like to try a new fishing venue. After what appeared to be a long drive in his car, we arrived at a quiet backwater used as a private mooring for Thames cruisers big and small. What awaited me when we arrived, took my breath away. The weather was autumnal perfection with warm still air and clear blue sky. The stunning colours of the tree leaves glistening in the sun with all shades of golden browns and yellows, combined with the scent of decaying leaves and the distinctive aromas of the riverbank is a scene that I will never forget. The smooth flowing river and the atmosphere of being close to the majestic and beautiful River Thames filled me with a sense of awe – and anticipation.

Bushnell's boatyard is situated on the outskirts of the small village of Wargrave. During the summer months the leisure boats occupied all the moorings but are lifted from the river and stored on the bank during the winter. As the winter lift hadn't started, John suggested I fished under the railway bridge while he had some business with the owner of the boatyard, Len Bushnell.

I walked across a narrow wooden footbridge to the island and started to cast my float into the quiet but shallow water under the brick arch of the railway bridge. This was the first time I had fished the River Thames which although clear, was full of 'fishy' features such as lily pads and gravel runs. With maggots as bait, the float settled, then immediately disappeared – and to my amazement I was staring at a plump, half-pound roach. Second cast, and another roach greedily devoured my hook bait. This was followed by a beautiful silver dace, a small chub, a perfectly striped perch, a large gudgeon, a ruffe and a small bream. Time stood still, and I was totally absorbed, elated by catching virtually all the species of fish that inhabit the Thames. The emotions live with me, even today.

However, to my great disappointment, John came to say it was time to go. On the way back to Bracknell, he mentioned that Len Bushnell had given me permission to fish his very private boatyard. Full of future expectations, I was an incredibly happy and excited boy that day.

My main fishing buddy was Frank, who would consistently regale me with tales of his fishing exploits on the Hampshire Avon with his father. When I recounted my day on the Thames at the boatyard, his ears pricked up and he suggested it would be a good idea if he could join me on my next outing. I could see that this was the beginnings of a symbiotic relationship. Here for Frank was an opportunity to raise the quality of his fishing to another level without the dependence on his father. For me, my angling had until now been confined to local ponds with limited potential. His experience and knowledge of fishing in rivers would give me a valuable insight and a boost to my angling technique. Another massive benefit for both of us would be the ability to fish in a super 'private' fishery without needing either of our parents' prior arrangements and transportation.

We now researched the best mode of travelling between Bracknell and Wargrave. Our options were limited, as we would be fully loaded down with our fishing gear.

Frank and I calculated that the best way to travel was by train: Bracknell to Reading – Reading to Twyford – Twyford to Wargrave

The small station at Wargrave was no more than a hundred yards from the backwater, which made it an ideal end and start for our rather torturous journey. We researched timetables, and often had only seconds to spare changing platforms loaded down with fishing boxes, rods, nets and buckets of ground bait. If we had an empty train carriage, our finest lobworms (6 inches in length before being fully extended) would be raced across the seat. On one occasion an elderly lady came into our compartment during a worm race. She turned around and walked out obviously disgusted, only to re-enter asking us for our names and the schools we attended. We lied politely when giving our details.

It became obvious that relying on public transport could only be a temporary solution. We had to find another way of travelling the 12 miles between Bracknell and Wargrave. A birthday present

Ready to set off for Wargrave

transformed my ability to travel: a Raleigh 3-speed bicycle. Frank and I modified our bikes to carry fishing boxes, ground bait (28 lb of breadcrumbs, flaked maize and bran), flasks and stacks of sandwiches; not to mention fishing gear, large umbrellas and sleeping bags – if we decided to stay overnight.

To fund my fishing, I started work for Engel, a German former prisoner of war. He had a successful landscape gardening business and provided my father with a second job. I was encouraged to give the gardening business a try. Initially my tasks involved nothing but weeding, which I found tedious and mind-numbingly boring. Once I graduated to working with Engel, learning the techniques involved in landscaping, the work became interesting and satisfying. Much of the '60s, during school half terms, holidays and occasional weekends would be spent helping him, mainly by supplying the back-breaking manual labour. I enjoyed being outside, working with the soil and doing something constructive. It also enabled me to afford to improve the quality of my fishing gear and associated essentials such as maggots and groundbait.

The hard work also had the benefit of improving my physique and strength, which became apparent in that all my sporting activities improved. Besides playing county rugby, I was also the county shot put champion from age 12 to 16. Often the competitors would be twice my size, so despite being of average height and weight for my age, I had the advantage of technique, speed and strength.

That autumn, Frank and I would be fishing the Thames at Wargrave at any opportunity. There was an increasing element of competitiveness creeping into our trips. On one notable occasion in late November, we were fishing on the island bank of the boatyard. The boat moorings were old and rotting with the wooden posts set parallel to the bank. Most of the resident boats had been lifted from their moorings to overwinter on dry land. This gave us the opportunity to fish many more swims and the moorings were very useful as rod rests and to suspend our keep nets. At that time, it was normal practice to retain all the fish that we caught until the end of the session. This gave us a means of comparing our respective catches before releasing them. Without this method of verification, the fish we caught would somehow morph into being recounted as bigger and heavier.

The fishing had been superb, and both of us had a net full of prime roach and dace. Frank had developed an annoying habit of wanting to see my catch before the end of the session. This entailed lifting my fish out of the water and disturbing my fishing. To get a view of my catch, Frank had straddled one foot on the bank and the other on the mooring post. Under Frank's considerable weight the post started moving. As if I was watching in slow motion, Frank's legs stretched wider and wider until the inevitable splash – and he was completely submerged in cold Thames muddy water.

We had become good friends due to our mutual love of fishing, but in those early days he did have some annoying habits.

Was I amused? Yes.

Was I annoyed? Yes. My fishing had been temporarily disrupted.

One of the boatyard workers saw what had happened and came across to help me fish Frank from the river. Besides being cold, he was covered from head to foot in river mud and slime. The kindly boatman arranged to dry Frank's clothes by a large paraffin heater which he wheeled out of the boathouse. Using the boathouse as shelter, Frank was not only warm and dry in his underpants but could also carry on fishing into the backwater on the opposite bank to me. He became so engrossed in his fishing that I had to point out that his socks and vest had caught fire whilst being draped over the heater.

Did this spoil our enjoyment of the day's fishing? Of course not.

Winter 1962–1963

December 1962 was a vintage time for me to enjoy village and youth club dances, especially with my increased interest in pop music and girls. I have always loved the atmosphere Christmas generates especially the feelings cultivated by carols such as 'Silent Night', 'O Little Town of Bethlehem' and 'O Come All Ye Faithful'. It was late on Christmas Eve, and having spent an enjoyable evening at the home of a girlfriend and her family, I sauntered home with a big smile on my face, humming 'White Christmas'. The mood transformed into another level of euphoria when it started to snow. The night was still, the silent snowflakes were huge and quickly created a beautiful white blanket. It was the perfect and magical start to Christmas that many of us dream of.

Waking up Christmas morning to a 12-inch-deep layer of snow, I was filled with thoughts of snowball fights and sledging. Little did I realise that this winter wonderland would be the norm for more than the next three months. Every night until mid-March there was either a deep frost or it snowed.

The extreme cold weather made most outdoor sporting activities almost impossible, including our fishing trips. I remember that winter as a time for indoor activities such as board and card games, playing with our model soldiers, watching television and listening to the radio. At that time only Frank's household had a record player, but the record selection belonged to his parents and was too old for us.

My nose

Christmas Day 1962 was really memorable, all the family together, a traditional turkey dinner and a superb lumberjack jacket as my present. However, I was constantly looking out to our garden and being fascinated by the beautiful unbroken carpet of deep snow. The snow was perfect for sledging. Next morning my estate friends were knocking on my door not wanting to discuss and compare our Christmas presents but to plan our winter 'sports activities'. Our focus was on building sledges, and in our case, that would be any object or material that could slide down the very steep Beech Hill. Today the slope would be regarded as treacherous and dangerous. Hazards included a very steep slope, trees, tree stumps, tree roots, wire fencing and other humans.

The 'piste' at Beech Hill, very quickly turned to sheet ice by the end of the day and became life-threatening, even by our standards. There were many casualties, but no hospitalisations. From day to day, fresh snowfall would renew and slow down the surface and keep the injury rate relatively low. Besides wooden sledges, we used planks of wood, prams without wheels and plastic sheets – but the most popular was a full-size wooden door. The door could carry four to six people and by the end of the 'piste', bodies would be strewn at various parts of the concourse.

On one occasion I followed the door to the bottom of the hill, on a super-fast sledge (the pram). At the bottom of the run, I crashed into the door which had been upended. The door fell on my head, flattening my nose. Copious amounts of blood added to the already blood-stained snow. I was not overly concerned until, on arriving home, my mother thought my nose had turned Roman – i.e. roaming over my face. My confidence at this age was not helped at the local hospital, a couple of weeks later, when the doctor's first comment was: 'What have you done to your nose, it's enormous!' I looked in the mirror and thought that it looked normal!

I asked the doctor if an operation could be considered to reduce its size and remodel it. My request was taken seriously, and I was referred to a consultant psychiatrist for a psych assessment. He sympathised with me over the enormity of my conk, then asked me if I had any friends or girlfriends. I unknowingly made the mistake of answering in the affirmative. 'Sorry, chum, you will have to live with it or pay privately for a nose job.' With the snow falling and my intention to play contact sports such as rugby, the likelihood of my conk being bashed again couldn't be discounted. Having met an attractive girl at a New Year dance who didn't seem concerned and made no comment about the size of my hooter, my confidence in my facial appearance was partially restored.

I decided that life was good despite my nose. And I still had my pop music!

* * *

On reflection, the dynamics of the early '60s pop scene – i.e., 1960–63 – was in a rapidly evolving formative phase. Previously, pop music was confined to relatively few artists, many of whom had not only been around for most of the 50's but also their songs were often in the 'charts' for months and years after they were first released. That's not to say there wasn't some great music in the '50s.

The Shadows – 'Wonderful Land' – Hank Marvin was an outstanding guitarist at the time and his movements around the stage memorable! Reminds me of the magical snowy winter.

Cliff Richard and The Shadows – 'I'm Looking Out the Window/ Do You Wanna Dance'

Chubby Checker – 'The Twist'/ 'Let's Twist Again' – Became a standard at dances, etc. throughout the early '60s.

The Tornados – 'Telstar' – Imagine a coach load of school kids on route to a game of rugby, all playing along to the tune with paper and combs.

Fritz Spiegl – 'Theme from Z-Cars' – Another paper and comb tune!

Little Eva – 'The Loco-Motion' – Another dance craze.

Mr Acker Bilk – 'Stranger on the Shore'

Neil Sedaka – 'Breaking Up is Hard to Do'

The Four Seasons – 'Sherry / Big Girls Don't Cry'

Contours – 'Do You Love Me'

Ray Charles – 'I Can't Stop Loving You'

Kenny Ball & his Jazzmen – 'Midnight in Moscow'

Brian Hyland – 'Ginny Come Lately'

Beach Boys – 'Surfin' Safari'. The start of the 'West Coast Sound'

Frank Ifield – 'I Remember You'

Pat Boone – 'Speedy Gonzales'

Carole King – 'It Might as Well Rain Until September'

And of course, the launch of the Beatles with 'Love Me Do'. Who would know how big 1963 would be for them!

1963

The year began with persistent cold, deep snow and frozen milk on the doorstep. Often the blue tits would peck through the silver foil to eat the cream. Here was a truly Nordic winter. In Bracknell and the surrounding districts, it was business and school as normal. If there had been snow days, we wouldn't have attended school for three months. On our housing estate everybody walked to school. The era of parents taking kids to school in Chelsea tractors had not arrived. My walk to school was over a mile, a time to chat about pop music, girls we fancied, and snowball fights.

In the countryside the snow laid deep and crisp and even, well into April. We realised that our native birds and all forms of wildlife had found it virtually impossible to survive month after month in such extreme conditions. As a country, we did lose huge numbers of our resident bird population from songbirds and corvids to raptors. Consequently, from that time forward, collecting birds' eggs became a complete no-no.

* * *

During this time listening to pop music became increasingly important part of my life. The extreme weather meant that my friends and I were spending a larger proportion of time confined to our homes. This period coincided with the appearance and dominance of the Beatles, Bob Dylan, the Beach Boys – and many more. The classic BBC programme *Juke Box Jury*, hosted by David Jacobs, was a must-see, even if the panellists were in our view mainly old farts.

Albums (LPs) started to gain huge importance. From my point of view, if an album contained a good number of great songs, it was more cost-effective than singles (although some 45s did have great B sides) – another good reason to buy the early Stones and Beatles LPs.

Some of my favourite albums of 1963:

The Beatles – *With the Beatles, Please Please Me*

The Beach Boys – *Surfin' USA, Little Deuce Coupe*

Roy Orbison – *In Dreams*

Dionne Warwick – *Presenting Dionne Warwick*

Cliff Richard – *Summer Holiday*. Started the year on top but quickly faded, mainly due to the dominance of the Beatles.

My singles selection:

The Beatles. – 'Please Please Me'/ 'Ask Me Why'
'I Want to Hold Your hand'/ 'This Boy'
'From Me to You'/ 'Thank You Girl
'She Loves You'/ 'I'll Get You', all number ones, with good B sides. Initially not impressed with their 'poppy image' their music was too good to ignore.

Rolling Stones – 'Come On'. I heard this single at a youth club and knew this was a group I would be following.

Gerry &The Pacemakers – 'You'll Never Walk Alone'
'I Like It'
'How Do You Do It'

Cliff Richard – 'Summer Holiday'
'The Next Time/Bachelor Boy'

The Rooftop Singers – 'Walk Right In'

Roy Orbison – 'In Dreams'. Great song; Fantastic voice.
'Blue Bayou'
'Falling'

Kathy Kirby – 'Secret Love' From the 1953 film *Calamity Jane*. The film starred and was sang by the fabulous Doris Day. Who didn't have a crush on her?

The Searchers – 'Sugar and Spice'
'Sweet For My Sweet'

Brian Poole & The Tremeloes – 'Do You Love Me?'
'Twist And Shout'

Trini Lopez – 'If I Had A Hammer'

Bobby Vee – 'The Night Has A Thousand Eyes'

The Ronettes – 'Be My Baby'. – This song made me fall in love with Motown.

Del Shannon – 'Little Town Flirt'.

Dave Clarke Five – 'Glad All Over'. One of the all-time foot stompers

The Springfields. – 'Island of Dreams'. Shows off Dusty's voice.

Dusty Springfield – 'I Only Want to Be with You'

Bob Dylan – 'Blowing in The Wind'

Peter Paul and Mary – 'Blowing in The Wind'

Beach Boys – 'Surfin' USA'

The Surfaris – 'Wipe Out'

Jan & Dean – 'Surf City'

During a local village dance, the performing group explained that they were playing "Surf music" also called "California sound".

Many of our records we played on Frank's Dansette record player until the needle or the grooves wore out; especially 'Glad All Over'. For a hormonal teenager, many of the songs created extraordinarily strong emotions and even today bring back poignant memories.

By the middle of May 1963, all the minor roads were clear of ice and the snow had melted. I was looking forward to the start of the coarse fishing season at one minute past midnight on the morning of 16 June. The target venue would be Bushnell's boatyard. Because of a school cricket match, I could not fish on the Saturday. Instead, we set off at 3 a.m. Sunday morning to catch the magical and productive first light. Casting a lobworm (a King William) under a boat moored to the opposite bank, led to a fantastic pull on my ledger rod. I had hooked into my target fish, a big chub. Thirty seconds later I was reeling in an empty hook. The air was blue with my expletives and Frank's gleeful comment: 'What a shame you didn't land it.' Having lost the only chance to catch a chub, we resorted to float fishing with masses of ground bait and maggots. We were both rewarded with a net full of lovely roach, dace, perch and a few small bream. A great start to the season.

On the way home, we would talk about the big one that got away and look forward to a drink in the Roebuck Pub. Although we were only 12 years old, we parked our bikes loaded with fishing gear outside the pub, and went inside, where the landlord had a pint of beer for Frank and a pint of cider for me, waiting on the bar. Because the landlord tolerated our presence in his pub, the Roebuck became the site for many drinking sessions in our early teenage years. Those were the days when underage drinking was common – if you knew where to go! The likelihood of being arrested for being drunk in charge of a bicycle was relatively low. The cost of drinking in pubs was affordable even for working-class urchins like us. A ten-bob note (or 50p today) would buy enough beer to make most hardened drinkers stagger home.

My family's summer holiday in 1963 was to the Isle of Sheppey. I was allowed to take Frank, and because the holiday camp was adjacent to the sea, we planned to try our arm at beach fishing. It is generally accepted that the further the bait can be cast out, the better the chances of catching fish. With that in mind, Frank and I would stand at one end of a local football pitch and practice our casting. Using our 10 ft sea rods, multipliers and a 4-ounce weight we both could cast over a hundred yards. To practice handling the expected massive fish we would catch, we asked some passing 5–6-year-olds to run off with our fishing lines and tried to reel them in. Nobody was injured.

The holiday was great fun, but the fishing was a disaster. No matter what we tried, all we could catch were small crabs. The disappointing results put us off trying beach fishing anywhere else in the UK. In fact, I cannot remember any follow up sea fishing trips for many years afterwards. I used my sea fishing gear for piking instead.

Because getting to the river at Wargrave was a substantial logistical exercise, we continued to fish local ponds such as Binnie Brickyard and some smaller ponds around Bracknell. Although further to cycle to, one of these ponds was our favourite because it contained only tench. These were no larger than a pound in weight, and spotting the distinctive small bubbles that indicated that they were active in our swims filled us with anticipation. The uniqueness of their soft smooth olive-green skin, a small red eye, a fighting quality and strength way above their actual weight made the fishing a truly memorable experience. I just love the species and even today I will travel many miles if there is a good chance of catching tench.

On one fine Sunday, I broke my own rule by inviting a girl to join me while I was fishing the tench pond. It was our first date, and she was more interested in passionate snogging, rather than the excellent tench fishing. I was enjoying the unique experience of deciding if my youthful carnal feelings were more powerful than my love of catching tench. However, the peace and tranquillity of my perfect afternoon was shattered by Frank. He suddenly turned up with a fishing hook deeply embedded in his pouted lower lip. The girlfriend was horrified by his appearance and was panicking about how we could help him. Looking at Frank, all I could think of was how he resembled a very large, hooked cod. He even had that same blank stare. The hook had a barb and would need to be surgically removed. I cut the hook from the trailing line and told him to go to the hospital to be unhooked by the professionals. Due to this untimely interruption, I couldn't recapture the passion of earlier that afternoon – and to cap it all, the tench had stopped biting.

The River Loddon at Winnersh was another fishing venue that became a firm favourite. One of our early ventures combined a camping trip with fishing. Once word of the proposed trip was circulated to our non-fishing estate friends, many of them decided to join us, bringing with them younger brothers and whatever primitive fishing gear that they could muster. Although the fun of camping was the main event, everybody was also trying various fishing spots along the bank. While trying to fish alone, Mathew, one of the juniors, started shouting that he had caught a whopper. Those of us who were in hearing range told him to shut up, the noise was spoiling the fishing. Eventually I decided to see what was going on.

Young Mathew was looking bemused as he sat on the riverbank with his legs dangling over the water, holding a short cane rod with a reel that had cotton as the line.

He looked at me and said, 'Honestly, Brian, it is really big.' My retort was to the effect that I really hoped this was not going to be a waste of my time. I peered into the river and directly below Mathew's Wellington boots was the head of a monster pike. The head alone was at least 12 inches long, and possibly as wide. The monster had grabbed a small fish that Mathew had caught and had semi-beached itself in the process of lunging for it. The monster pike – or should I have called it a crocodile? – stared up at me and suggested that it was my move. Who was more frightened? Yes, it was me.

To this day, I am still left wondering what I could have done differently. By now a small crowd had gathered to observe the situation. Although the huge pike was within reach of our landing nets, none of us had a net big enough to even partly contain it. Could we try to haul the beast out with our hands? Given that the fish was fresh and armed with needle-sharp teeth, none of us were either brave or stupid enough to try to grab the fish by its head and drag it onto the bank. After about five minutes of stalemate, the pike (obviously bored) decided to reverse its way back into the river and slowly swam away, not being aware of the cotton line snapping.

Later we estimated the pike would have weighed at least 25 lb, and despite future attempts to catch it from that swim, with suitable tackle, the monster from the deep was never seen again. That stretch of the river became another favourite of ours that summer and autumn, especially for prime roach and dace, caught with maggots, hemp and elderberry.

The Loddon is a tributary of the Thames and by sheer coincidence joins it just upstream of Bushnell's boatyard. Both rivers are full of beautiful plump roach, a fish that even today we love to catch. To be float fishing on the river, getting bites, radio playing quietly, eating a sandwich and sipping a cup of flask tea or coffee is *bliss*. Besides enjoying the environment, especially by these rivers, we accumulated a huge amount of angling knowledge from the more experienced fishermen that we encountered fishing close by. I have always appreciated the camaraderie of anglers who will share their knowledge and experiences. There will always be of tales of fish caught that got away.

That summer, trips involving camping and fishing became our most fun pastime. To be close to water and experience the mist and smells of the summer, the sun rising at dawn, the excitement of the best of early morning fishing and the fading light of the evening was magic. Much later I learned that early mornings and evenings as day turns to night is when the fish feed voraciously.

Even when our outings involved kids younger than ourselves, our parents didn't appear concerned or worried and I cannot remember any of us being asked to be careful. How times have changed.

When the question of looking back to my life in 1963 and considering how much was I affected by teenage angst, my reply would be by an insignificant amount (even allowing for my nose). My life was about school, work, sport, fishing, local village dances and Cooper's Hill Youth Club. Even most evenings were filled with amazing pop music and meeting girls from school and the youth club. This meant that there was truly little time to mope around. Listening to the blues and folk songs by the greats such as Bob Dylan, 'Blowin' in the Wind'; Rolling Stones 'I Wanna Be Your Man'; Roy Orbison 'In Dreams'; Joan Baez 'We Shall Overcome'; and of course, the Beatles gave meaning to music that transformed my 12-year-old self.

'Goin' Back' by Dusty Springfield epitomises why I love the innocence of those early years of the '60s. Although I place snippets of the song throughout my book, please listen to the words of this lovely song in its entirety.

Michaelmas term was when I made a breakthrough in my sporting prowess. I captained the U-13s school rugby and was selected to play rugby for the county, Berkshire. Even when there were matches on a Saturday, Frank and I had an open invite to join his father and his mates for a couple of pints at the Golden Farmer. All the drinks were provided free. This was fine, except the afternoons often involved competitive rugby matches for Bracknell Colts. Once or twice, I may have played under the influence. Later I realised that drinking alcohol was better imbibed after a match.

Assassination of John F Kennedy 23 November 1963

A few of us were visiting our old primary school fete, when over a loudspeaker came the announcement of the assassination of John F Kennedy. Even at 13, I realised something tragic, and shocking had taken place. For many years afterwards, we agree that we could all recall what we were doing ,when JFK was murdered. I had been enjoying a lovely warm sunny November afternoon talking to and mingling with past friends at a school fête, but on hearing this news we were all stunned and distressed.

Sometimes, I wish that returning to the relative innocent days of childhood when we were only concerned with day- to- day living was still possible.

Bear

Just before Christmas 1963 I received an offer for my egg collection from a school mate, who we nicknamed Bear. For the sum of five pounds, he had purchased forty-eight pristine different British Birds eggs, displayed on white cotton wool, in a cardboard box. Together with the Herring gull, I rated my pale blue Redstart's egg the pride of the collection. Bear was delighted to have my unique collection, and I had funds for Christmas. Bear was in the same class as me and often we would walk to school together. He was a loner, but I liked him. We would often listen for hours to the fantastic Goons. The long-running *Goon Show* starred comic geniuses such as Spike Milligan, Peter Sellers, Harry Secombe and Michael Bentine. The plots were ridiculous with dim humour, puns, sound effects and songs. Both the Beatles and Monty Python were influenced by the Goons. We would often try to imitate the voices of Neddie Seagoon, Eccles and Moriarty.

Bear and I were of similar academic levels, so we would often share homework answers.

Bear was a pathetic angler, and it took a lot of persuading for the others, especially Frank, to allow him to join us at Wargrave.

On the first occasion that Bear fished in the backwater, I equipped him with my crudest tackle and told him to sit outside the boathouse and dangle a small worm close to the bank. It was a tactic to keep him from disturbing and mucking up our fishing. He wondered around looking at the boats and stood behind us asking us how we were doing. Not the dedication and focus we were hoping for. I politely asked him to return to his swim and persevere. A few minutes later Bear asked if I could bring the landing net, as he had caught a fish. Irritated, Frank disdainfully shouted, 'You don't need a net, just lift it out of the water!' By this time, I was standing next to Bear, looking into the water at a huge trout. It did indeed need a landing net, as we estimated that this once in a lifetime Thames brown trout weighed at least 3 lb. Len Bushnell came out of the boathouse office to find out what the commotion was all about. The question rapidly arose around what we were going to do with the fish.

Bear, to his great credit, offered the fish to Len, who had the reputation of being a no-nonsense kind of person. To our surprise he accepted the catch with genuine gratitude. This was a master stroke, as the backwater was strictly for moorings only, and we often felt we had been pushing our luck to be fishing there regularly. Now Len informed us we could come and fish the backwater whenever we liked without having to ask.

Thank you, Bear.

The autumn and winter of 1963 was a time with few hassles or concerns. Yes, my mother suggested that girls wouldn't be attracted to me because of my big nose and my receding hairline raised some doubts, but I really couldn't have cared less. I was enjoying school, sports, friends – and despite my mum's opinion, various girls found me attractive enough to go out with me. Even the weekend's boring job of weeding the massive flowerbeds of the Met Office HQ in Bracknell didn't dampen my enjoyment of life. To make the job bearable, I now had the luxury of my trusty transistor radio turned to full volume to help pass my work time. Plus, any period of clement weather suitable for fishing just added to my perception of a utopian life.

Financially, with careful budgeting I could afford to enjoy my lifestyle activities. My parents considered me too old and self-reliant to continue receiving pocket money. Although a fair bit of cash was taken the few weeks before Christmas, this was the last year of industrial carol singing: as choristers, we were no longer young or angelic.

1964

Like many teenagers who possessed a small transistor radio, Sunday evening was an important moment. Between 11 p.m. and midnight was Radio Luxembourg's Top 20 Pop chart, starting for some reason with the Number 1 and going into reverse through the chart's placings. With school next morning, I developed a technique for secret listening to avoid incurring the wrath of my parents: I placed a pillow over my head with the radio turned up as loud as possible. Although the reception of Radio 208 was often erratic, it kept me up to date and therefore cool.

Many of the famous disc jockeys started their career with Radio Luxembourg, including Jimmy Young, Alan Freeman, Simon Dee, Kenny Everett, Brian Mathews, Hughie Green and Katie Boyle.

Top of the Pops started on BBC television and, although in black and white, enabled us to actually see the acts that were generating all the new pop music.

Radio Caroline was launched on 28 March. With all-day pop music, Simon Dee, Tony Blackburn, Jonnie Walker, Dave Lee Travis and Emperor Rosko became household names, especially with a new generation of pop lovers. Tony Blackburn opened the first show with 'Rag Doll' by Frankie Valli and the Four Seasons onboard the boat that was Radio Caroline. Now we could listen to music all day and night. With a much-improved reception, my transistor radio was becoming an essential part of my fishing trips, dates with girls and leisure time with my mates.

* * *

1964 was when many of the words of songs, dare I say the poetry in them, started to have a profound emotional impact on me. Even as a 13-year-old I realised that this was the start of an incredibly special era of music, and I am so grateful to have been a part of that special time. Because of the huge number of new songs being released the list of my favourites is becoming more extensive and diverse.

Beatles 'If I Fell" – one of their best love songs.
'I Want to Hold Your Hand'
'She Loves You'
'Hard Day's Night'
'Please Please Me'
'Can't Buy Me Love.' With the phenomenon of Beatle mania, the second half of 1964 was completely dominated by the 'Fab Four'.

Roy Orbison – 'Oh Pretty Woman'; 'It's Over' – my favourite of OB's.

The Beach Boys – 'I Get Around'. Classic west coast freewheeling song.

Supremes – 'Baby Love' – With Diana Ross's voice, I loved this song the moment I heard it.

Rockin' Berries – 'He's in Town'

Kinks – 'All Day & All of the Night'; 'You Really Got Me' – both great and timeless rock songs.

Dionne Warwick – 'Walk on By'

The Four Seasons – 'Rag Doll'; One of my all-time favourites and was Tony Blackburn's first record to be played on Radio Caroline.

Searchers – 'Needles and Pins'; 'Don't Throw Your Love Away'

The Animals – 'The House of the Rising Sun' – Great version sung by Eric Burdon

The Dave Clark Five – 'Bits and Pieces'; 'Glad All Over' – Frank and I played would this endlessly.

Hollies – 'I'm Alive'

Cilla Black – 'You're My World' and 'Anyone Who Had a Heart'. Cilla's voice at its best.

Petula Clark – 'Down Town' – so atmospheric.

Rolling Stones – 'It's All Over Now'; 'Little Red Rooster', 'Time is On My Side' – This was my style of music.

Righteous Brothers – You've Lost that Loving Feeling' – a classic.

Zombies – 'She's Not There' featuring the great voice of Colin Blunstone.

Swinging Blue Jeans – 'Hippy Hippy Shake'

The Who – 'I can't Explain'

Moody Blues – 'Go Now' – classic. Deserved being number one in the charts.

Bob Dylan – 'The Times They Are a-Changin'. All about the message.

Simon & Garfunkel – 'Sound of Silence'. Mind-blowing song for me.

Them – including Van Morrison – 'Gloria'. I couldn't wait for it to come on the radio.

Nashville Teens – 'Tobacco Road'. Great.

Gene Pitney – 'Twenty Four Hours from Tulsa'. Such a good singer, such a good story.

Gerry and the Pacemakers – 'Don't Let the Sun Catch You Crying' – just great.

To sit fishing in the backwater at Wargrave with my radio and quietly singing along to many of the above was, as we would say at the time, fab. I suppose that today we would call it living in the moment.

Tales of rebellious behaviour coming from popular rock groups such as the Rolling Stones, Kinks and the Who only made them more attractive.

Rather than put me off these groups, the negative publicity inspired my first album purchase – *The Rolling Stones*, their first UK album with Decca Records. I got to know the words of every song – 'Route 66', 'I Just Want to Make Love to You', 'Carol', 'Tell Me (You're Coming Back)', *et al.*, and the amazing guitar playing on 'I'm a King Bee'. I was a Stones convert. My limited record collection and appreciation only increased with the release of their albums *Rolling Stones No. 2* and *Aftermath*. On reflection, some of my attitudes towards girls at the time were also being influenced by the Rolling Stones' words and song themes.

1964 was historically significant:

Martin Luther King Jr was awarded the Nobel Peace Prize. He donated the $54,123 prize money to aid the Civil Rights Movement.

Nelson Mandela was sentenced to life imprisonment.

USA started active involvement in Vietnam.

Abolition of the death penalty in UK.

In sport, boxing became prominent in the media. Cassius Clay ('Float like a butterfly, Sting like a bee') became the World Heavyweight Champion by beating Sonny Liston. As my father was a boxing fan for many years, Clay became a conversation topic for both of us to discuss.

Radio, television and newspapers were becoming an ever-important source of everything that would influence my developing young psyche. However, I also started to mentally note that an application of healthy scepticism should be applied to most 'facts' being presented to the public at large.

Still, my hyperactive life meant that I paid attention to the media influences only when I couldn't think of much else to do – these moments were mercifully rare.

School cricket matches were played on Saturday afternoons during the summer term. I was a middle order batsman and had a good throwing arm. I enjoyed playing cricket, but it was time-consuming – and time involved in a match was less time fishing. As soon as the last ball was bowled, I was off home ASAP.

As our fishing trips, especially to Wargrave, were becoming longer and often overnight, planning was of great importance. There was all the fishing tackle, bait, groundbait and clothing, but we gave priority to food and beverages. Flasks of tea, coffee and water were essential to wash down our home-prepared sandwiches. I loved Shippam's salmon paste with cucumber. Even today, a fishing trip is not complete without sandwiches and a drink (preferably hot).

Fact: When coarse fishing, any seasoned angler will tell you that the time to have a cup of tea/coffee is when the fishing slows, and the fish stop biting. However, with a cup of hot tea in one hand and a sandwich in the other, it is inevitable that you will get the best bite of the day and miss it! This would be followed by spilling tea and maggots and a bout of extreme swearing. Some things in life will never change.

Although we loved the boatyard from an angling viewpoint, the moorings were rotting, rickety and unsafe. They were also shallow due to years of silting up. Often when one of the larger boats moved, they would churn up a mass of mud and weed although this would make little difference to the quality of the fishing.

Then, in mid-October, we arrived at first light on a Sunday morning to find a huge barge/dredger parked in our usual fishing spot. Undeterred, we set up our fishing gear and took advantage of the position the barge had been left moored in mid water and made a superb fishing platform. With all the disturbances to the delicate ecosystem of the backwater the question in our minds was: 'Will we get a bite, let alone a fish?'

After throwing in a few large handfuls of ground bait (flake maize/bran, bought at the pet food shop), Frank and I, side by side, sent our floats downstream and hoped for the best. We were not disappointed. Both floats slipped under the surface, and soon our keepnets were filling with quality roach and dace. As the day progressed, instead of the fishing slowing, it just got better. Bigger fish, but also a species we had not caught before – big bream. In those days to catch a bream of 2–4 lb became another level of achievement and excitement. Pike and big perch were also active – what a day! Dredging the backwater would continue for many months and despite all the disruption, the fishing was some of the best that I can remember. In fact, it was during this period that I caught my only specimen fish – a fish that weighs over 50% of the official record weight for that species.

November brought serious flooding to the Thames. I decided that the backwater was worth a try despite the mud from the dredging and the river being level with the bank. Armed with my transistor radio, I reckoned that even if the fishing was poor, the music was going to be great, and so it proved. 'If I Fell', 'Rag Doll', 'Down Town' were among my favourites, played one after another – bliss. The river was brown, fast and extremely high. My only option was to fish so close to the bank that I could literally pour bucketloads of ground bait into where the fish may be sheltering. I used large lobworms (King Williams) for bait. The fishing was slow as expected, when suddenly, after a viscous tug of my rod tip, I was playing a large bream – or so I thought. When it came to the surface and flashed a side of green, red and silver, I realised the fish was either a very large roach or rudd. The fish shook its head and came off the hook. After the usual swearing, I tried again. Within a minute, after another great bite, a fish similar but smaller was safely landed on the bank. To my great pleasure and surprise, I was staring at an enormous roach. It weighed 2lb 1oz and is to this day the largest roach I have seen or caught since.

The Kinks were playing 'You Really Got Me': I was glowing with pride and self-satisfaction; in that moment life couldn't have been better.

Other out-of-school activities

Cooper's Hill Youth Club became another regular venue for my out-of-school activities as even I had to admit I needed to broaden my horizons. Besides the constant playing of up-to-date records, discos, table tennis, billiards/snooker and the usual social interactions with friends, several outings were arranged. Through the Youth club I entered orienteering and athletics competitions, and target shooting with .303 rifles at Sandhurst Military Academy. Unlike school, my new group of friends both male and female, didn't judge me by my age which was fortunate because I was often hankering after some of the attractive older girls. Sometimes this attraction was reciprocated – a recipe for trouble, but that's another story.

Fashion was creeping into my perception. With truly little funds, my clothes were not exactly Carnaby St, but as my father worked for a clothing company, I would often wear my school trousers – i.e. my drainpipes, the ones that were greatly admired by the sixth form boys – to discos and dances. Haircuts were difficult to modify from that prescribed and strictly enforced short back and sides by my school. By now, I had a Boston and a short fringe mimicking the Mod style but wasn't allowed to grow my hair over my ears.

For the local village hall and youth club dances, I could count as hip. However, in the nearby town of Windsor, the legendary Ricky-Tick Club was attracting bands such as the Yardbirds, the Pretty Things, the Rolling Stones, The Who, Jimi Hendrix, Pink Floyd and Cream. Little wonder they wouldn't give entry to a bunch of underage under-dressed estate kids who had cycled from Bracknell to Windsor – despite the fact that we had hidden our pedal bikes before queuing up at the door. At least the bouncers were polite.

Even at the age of 13, I realised that 1964 could be regarded as a time when momentous changes were happening to society, especially the rise and influence of a younger generation – later to be labelled as the counterculture. Fashion, music, dancing, films, TV shows and even haircuts were being focused on a younger socioeconomic grouping. I was noticing the advertising of the day referred to sex, booze, clothing, fast cars and all that is associated with the rock and roll lifestyle; my wish was to have a bit of the action!

I was fortunate enough to attend a school where there were equal numbers of boys and girls. Together with dances, the Wimpy coffee bar and the youth club, I had opportunities to make new friends. In 1964, my own chat-up line, like so many other teenagers, was: 'Do you prefer the Beatles to the Stones?' 'What do you think of the latest songs from Bob Dylan or Simon and Garfunkel?' Heated debates would follow. How lucky was I that there were so many new and exciting genres of music to discuss and that it was almost universally of interest for my generation. Talking about fishing exploits, politics or the condition of the school rugby pitch wasn't going to hack it with most girls.

1964 was a year of great awakenings and expectations for me. Of course, like most teenagers, I had my disappointments and emotional down times. One of my biggest regrets of that time occurred on a particularly wet Sunday afternoon. A good-looking mate of mine and I had arranged to meet the two best-looking girls from our class. I had high hopes that this could be the start of a serious relationship.

After having lunch with my family on a particularly rainy Sunday, I told my parents that I was meeting some friends from school. My mother insisted that I would have to wear my school raincoat and Wellington boots. When I met my classmates, their looks said it all. Besides feeling uncool and ashamed, I was also completely ignored by the girl I fancied. You can't win 'em all. I should have gone fishing.

1965

Fishing was still my number one pastime. That said, the pub and associated alcoholic consumption were starting to feature more prominently in my leisure activities. Besides our Sunday visitation to The Roebuck, after a hard day and night's fishing at Wargrave, a regular mid-week session with my estate mates often included Frank. A 10-bob note (50p) each would be enough to make a 20-minute walk to the pub turn into an hour's slog to get home. Many a time, our parents wondered where we obtained flowers, bits of hedgerow, garden gnomes or scratches, or lost items of clothing. Often any memory of the previous night's activities had been lost in the ether of ethanol. A pint of beer in 1965 averaged 1 shilling, and there were 20 shillings to the pound sterling – in other words, a pint cost 5p!

The yard of ale

Opposite the long driveway to my secondary school stood the Black Horse pub. Pleasant enough décor, but above the bar hung a yard of ale vessel – a glass tube 3 ft long with a wider bulb at the blind end. The record for non-stop drinking of the entire two and half pints was 1 minute 18 seconds. The Black Horse was a drinker's pub which we occasionally frequented in the evenings. Frank, Richard and I were having a quiet pint when the bartender asked if any of us younger persons would like to try an attempt on the record. The reward was free drinks for the whole pub for the rest of the evening.

I declined the invitation, but Richard and Frank were up for the challenge. Richard was now my fishing buddy as well as being a classmate. Every morning at the school's break we would regularly drink three bottles of milk, each 1/3 pint. These were free, but most kids didn't drink their state-donated ration of milk. Richard and I thought that by drinking more ourselves the school could avoid wastage! Instead of drinking his milk like any normal person, Richard would literally tip the contents down his throat in less than a second. I now believe he was in practice for his time at Birmingham University, when he became the fastest pint of beer champion in the West Midlands.

A hush descended in the Black Horse as Richard started downing the contents of the yard of ale in an astonishingly fast time. Ten seconds gone, and the beer was down to the bowl. The record would be trashed. However, Richard has always been a messy eater and drinker and before long beer was not dribbling but pouring from the side of his mouth and from his nose. Clothes, shoes and body were soaked through and Richard was duly disqualified. My best prospect had failed, but Frank was known as a volume man.

When Frank started with his yard, the pub crowd showed little interest, especially after Richard's attempt. Quietly and at an even pace, Frank, after 40 seconds had less than one quarter of the bowl to go. Silence and wonderment reigned, then cheers of 'Come on, my lad, you can do it' rang through the pub. To everyone's surprise and disappointment, an amazing spectacle occurred. Frank hesitated, stopped drinking, took a deep breath, which was shortly followed by a deep gurgling and heaving. The yard of ale via Frank's mouth, as if by magic, completely refilled with beer and partially digested pork pie. After a few groans of disappointment and disgust from the assembled pub audience, we decided to make a quick exit after paying for the beer that had been wasted.

At school, Richard and I would discuss the amazing pop scene of 1965. New musical bands were appearing from towns and villages up and down the country. Eventually, with two other classmates, we formed our own band, called Grimble. Richard was about average on guitar and I was below average as a singer and bongo player. Although the other two were mediocre, our ambition was to improve by practice, and introduce a fantastic hit song that was playing all over Scandinavia and Europe, called 'Cadillac', by a group unknown in England, the Hep Stars.

NOTE. The Swedish rock group Hep Stars had a certain Benny Andersson as their keyboard player; and after he left the Hep Stars in the late '60s, he went on with Bjorn Ulvaeus to form a group called ABBA – the rest is history.

With a limited repertoire and very little confidence, Grimble was not quite as successful as we hoped for, and after about a year of rehearsing we could only perform a half-decent version of 'For Your Love' (by the Yardbirds) and Cadillac. After performing nil gigs, except in front of parents and girlfriends, we decided that we would have a rock star's lifestyle without the hassle of recording and performing – but also without as much money.

* * *

The abundance of all time pop music classics of 1965 has left a real and emotional imprint on my memory banks. Many of the songs encapsulated how and what I was feeling relating to my 'position in life':

'Poor Man's Son' (The Rockin' Berries)

'We Gotta Get Out of This Place' and 'It's My Life' (The Animals)

'My Generation' (The Who)

'King of the Road' (Roger Miller)

'Nowhere Man' (Beatles) – such clever words.

Songs which appealed to a new generation of ambitious wannabes – like me.

'Eve of Destruction' (Frank McGuire) reflected the mood of many people at the time and there was major concern regarding the rapidly escalating Vietnam War, the major conflict (war) between India and Pakistan, and the ever-present possibility of nuclear conflict between Russia and USA.

The BBC pulled 'The War Games', a programme about the aftermath of a nuclear war, over concerns that it was too frightening.

Although 'Ban the Bomb' and its associated rallies had been running for years, 1965 was the start of the really large-scale protest movements. In the USA, Dr Martin Luther King took part in a peaceful march from Selma Alabama to Montgomery in aid of civil rights, and Anti-Vietnam War demonstrations took place in Washington.

The controversial Malcolm X was assassinated on 21st February in Manhattan after returning from the UK. Earlier that month, Frank and I had decided to attend an advertised disco in Reading town hall. The venue was crawling with police – to prevent, we thought, the usual punch-ups between Mods and Rockers. We started to feel a little uncomfortable when a section of the dance hall was filled with sinister, zombie-looking, blue uniformed heavies that appeared to have just left the set of *Dr No* or a horror movie. We decided to ask a friendly police officer what was going on, only to be advised to leave fairly sharpish as Malcolm X and his henchmen were holding court. Glad I never met him.

Talking of villains, Ronnie and Reggie Kray were arrested and imprisoned. Ronnie Biggs (Great Train Robbery) promptly escaped from Wandsworth, to spend the next 34 years on the run, mainly in Argentina.

1965 saw the abolition of the Death Penalty.

The word 'fuck' was first spoken on British TV by Kenneth Tynan.

Pizza Express opened their first restaurant.

My personal hero of recent history, Winston Churchill, died 24th January aged 90 years.

BP strikes natural gas in the North Sea.

USA escalates the war in Vietnam by bombing virtually everything it could.

Kecksburg UFO. A fireball was seen travelling from Michigan to Pennsylvania with pictures of 'spacecraft' and encounters shown in local news outlets. Media blackout until 2005.

On the fashion front, Mary Quant, Twiggy and Jean Shrimpton started their respective careers. [Dame] Mary Quant popularised the miniskirt, surprisingly named after the Mini car – not the length of the skirt

Most people of my era would agree that 1965 was arguably, the best year for popular music ever.

Beatles

It was a momentous year; accumulating in being awarded MBEs. Besides releasing a string of great singles such as 'Michelle', 'Nowhere Man', 'Yesterday', 'Help', 'Ticket to Ride', 'I Feel Fine', 'Day Tripper/We Can Work It Out'.

Film – *Help!*

Albums – *Rubber Soul, Help, Beatles '65, Beatles VI.* I was becoming a begrudging admirer of the Beatles and secretly enjoyed their films.

The Rolling Stones

Because of their type of rock music, rebellious image and behaviour, I regarded the Stones as my favourite band of that year. '*Rolling Stones 1*', '*Rolling Stones 2*' and later '*Aftermath*'; were the core of my small collection.

Many of the tracks from these albums, just blew me away. I would know all the words to all the songs of every track. The records would be played so repetitively that my family's newly acquired Dansette record player was constantly in use, and the needles wore out quickly, as did the grooves in the records. 1965 wasn't too bad a year for Stones singles as well.

> 'The Last Time', 'Satisfaction', 'Get Off Of My Cloud', '19th Nervous Breakdown'. 'As Tears Go By'. 'Mother's Little Helper', 'Play With Fire', 'Time Is On My Side'. 'You Better Move On', 'Route 66'

The output of the Beatles and Stones alone would have filled the charts in most years, but in 1965 there were so many other fantastic artistes/songs that it was difficult for my teenage mind to take them all in. I will mention some that have a particular significance for me.

> 'Go Now' – The Moody Blues: Our school music teacher 'Dishy Dave' played 'Go Now' to the class's delight, and then set about rubbishing the structure and composition. Huge boos and rubbers were thrown at him.

I remember smashing bricks and rubble for Engel's house extension and listening to:

> 'Here Comes the Night'. Them (Van Morrison). Loved this song and as a bonus the record had 'Gloria' on the 'B' side.
>
> '(I'm A) Road Runner' – Jr Walker & the All-Stars. Resonated as our theme of being free and uncommitted.
>
> 'Satisfaction', 'The Last Time', 'Play with Fire' – Rolling Stones. At the time, I loved the attitude of the words to these songs.

I was becoming increasingly dependent on my transistor radio and would take it everywhere with me – work, rest, play, and school (during breaks).

The following songs, when in the company of young ladies, the music and words would help to set a 'romantic' mood – at least for me!

> 'In The Midnight Hour' – Wilson Pickett. Another all-time great.
>
> 'My Girl' – The Temptations. Many a great smooch to this song.
>
> 'Yesterday' – Matt Monro. What a voice – what a song.
>
> 'Unchained Melody' – The Righteous Brothers. Just an amazing version.
>
> 'Ferry Cross the Mersey', 'You'll Never Walk Alone' – Gerry and the Pacemakers. All time classics. Gerry's super soulful voice.
>
> 'Stop in the Name of Love' – The Supremes.
>
> 'I Got You Babe' – Sonny & Cher.
>
> 'Michelle' – Beatles.
>
> 'Under the Boardwalk' – Rolling Stones.
>
> 'Downtown' – Petula Clark.
>
> 'Concrete and Clay' – Unit 4 & 2.

'For Your Love', 'Heart Full of Soul' – The Yardbirds. The origin band of great artistes such as Eric Clapton, Jeff Beck and Jimmy Page.

'It's the Same Old Song', 'I Can't Help Myself [Sugar Pie Honey Bunch]' – Four Tops. Music to sing along and dance to.

There were many songs that resonated with my perceived position in life.

'Poor Man's Son' – The Rockin' Berries.

'We Gotta Get Out of This Place', 'It's My Life', 'Don't Let Me Be Misunderstood' – The Animals.

'Nowhere Man' – Beatles.

'My Generation', 'Any Way, Anyhow, Anywhere', 'I Can't Explain' – The Who.

'King Of the Road' – Roger Miller.

'A World of Our Own', 'The Carnival Is Over' – The Seekers.

'Eve of Destruction' – Frank McGuire. A song of today.

'Tired Of Waiting for You ', 'All Day All of the Night' – Kinks. Great rock songs that I never get tired of enjoying.

Bob Dylan – 'The Times They Are A-Changin', 'Positively 4th Street', 'Like A Rolling Stone'. Great songs with meaningful words; ropey voice.

The Byrds – 'Mr Tambourine Man'. 'All I Really Want To Do'. Both Bob Dylan songs but sung with great harmonies.

So many artists were starting their careers in 1965, such as Simon & Garfunkel. I spent many hours in the front room of a girlfriend's house and getting to know all the words to all the songs from the *Sounds of Silence* album.

Looking back, I instinctively knew that this was a time that popular music was not only coming of age but was part of a cultural revolution. For me the music was creating a 'reality' and perception that was to shape my formative years. Often people look back to their teenage years and say reflectively that they were the 'Good Old Days'. Without any hesitation, and it's not looking back with rose-coloured glasses, this *was* a great time for me.

> 'I can recall a time
> When I wasn't ashamed to reach out to a friend
> And now I think I've got
> A lot more than a skipping rope to lend'
> 'Goin' Back'

The car came off best

Living on a housing estate, I had a group of friends who were within a five-minute walk of each other. One friend, John, would normally walk to my house, but on one occasion it was raining, so he decided to use his bicycle. Head down and frantically peddling against wind and rain, he hit a parked car head on – literally. Most people would rollover the handlebars and instinctively roll up, but not John. Flying through the air like an eagle, he hit the car with his mouth – wide open as if to devour it. Undaunted, he continued his journey to my house and rang the front doorbell. I was met with the sight of my friend covered in blood and holding a handful of teeth. My first comment: 'Was it a blue car that you hit with your mouth?' Through a bloody gargle, John enquired how I knew. 'There's blue paint on your remaining front teeth.' When I accompanied John back to his home, it was easy to spot the offending car, as it had distinct teeth marks and blood on the bonnet. There were a few of his teeth scattered on the ground.

Within close range of my home there were five or six lads, all of a similar age and with similar interests: fishing, music, outings to the pub, and meeting girls. The additional bonus for me was that between them, they had extensive knowledge in different genres of music which I hadn't encountered before: R&B, Folk, Blues, Rock, Country, Folk and all genres. Without spending time with John and Dave, I would probably not have got to know some of the great Blues masters such as John Lee Hooker, Howlin' Wolf and Muddy Waters. Many of the great groups that emerged in the '60s such as

John Mayall & the Bluesbreakers and of course the Rolling Stones were heavily influenced by these early American legends.

We spent or possibly misspent many long winter evenings playing cards. Avoiding intellectual games such as Bridge, we chose various forms of Poker or Bragg. To make life interesting these games were played for money and could go on for hours, sometimes all night. We played for pennies, but often the pot could reach a pound or two. As our skill levels were fairly even, winnings would be evenly divided over a period of time between the regular players. If we felt a little strapped, Jim was invited to play.

Winter has traditionally been regarded as the time to catch pike and in the late autumn, Virginia Water became a potential new fishery with the anticipation of some good winter fishing ahead. It was a fabulous place to walk around as the lake is vast. Even today it's worth a visit to see the unique landscape and designs of Capability Brown and the Indian totem pole.

Over the Christmas period I decided to explore some new fishing spots. One of them was in a restricted area of the lake. I came across two Polish guys fishing a secluded bay, and their tackle suggested that they were pike fishing. Asking if they had caught anything, there was a shaking of their heads. At that moment, behind me there was a rustling of leaves and to my astonishment they had hidden two very large pike and a specimen perch. These fish were destined for the pot. Although they were fishing illegally, I decided to say nothing but was determined give this venue a try.

Reporting my findings to Richard, we quickly hatched a plan of attack to maximise our chances of catching pike. In very cold weather – and this particular weekend was bitter – bait fish like roach and dace would be very difficult to catch in a lake. So, on the Saturday we fished the river at Wargrave, and struggled to catch, even in the backwater. Eventually we managed eight bleak – a small silvery pest of a fish that under normal conditions we would have avoided like the plague. Richard stayed overnight with me in Bracknell, my parents kindly letting us keep the live fish in the bath all night. They all survived, only to be used as bait next day.

Although conditions were Arctic, our excitement was palpable as we watched a large float give a gentle bob, instantly making us forget the cold. Was it the live bleak getting excited and trying to swim away from an approaching predator, or was it a huge predator sampling its prey? The answer quickly became apparent when the float glided smoothly along the surface of the lake. We knew that this was now the start of a pike run. After what seemed to be an eternity, the bung disappeared under the surface and wallop, I struck into the fish. At this stage we did not know if the predator was 2 lb or 32 lb. This one was 2lb (you can't win 'em all), but the adrenaline rush was awesome. By midday, we had caught four pike. Although the biggest was just 5 lb, the excitement of this type of predator fishing remains until today. We now fish with dead fish baits.

During the next few years, we would return to Virginia Water, making it a regular winter pike venue.

During the summer months, our fishing trips to Shiplake, which is on the opposite bank to the boatyard, often involved staying overnight. As most course anglers will agree, the best fishing both for atmospherics and quality of sport is just as darkness falls and at first light in the morning. Midsummer would mean having daylight until nearly 11 p.m. and being able to catch first light at 4 a.m. Normally we would try to fish all through the night with an occasional upright nap. By the time the fishing slowed, which was usually by mid-morning, tiredness would hit me, and my eyes would cross or close, especially with the soporific effects of a gentle breeze, summer sun and fluffy clouds. I would often fall asleep sitting holding my rod, only to be awakened by a sharp tug of a fish biting.

Did we catch any more during these all-night sessions? – yes and no. Bigger roach, perch, dace, large eels, and the occasional chub but not always the numbers. Occasionally we would fish upstream of Shiplake weir. In the middle of the night – that is, between 1.30 a.m. and 3.30 a.m. – we would get a long slow pull on our bite indicator, a dough bobbin suspended from our line, our favourite method for detecting bites in the dark. When we connected with the fish that were giving us these unusual bites, there would be little movement or they would slowly charge upstream and despite all efforts, snap our line. It was like trying to catch an underwater monster. What were these leviathans that always got away? The extra frustration was that on most occasions we had only that single bite and opportunity for the whole of the night. Recently, giant river carp of over 30 lb have been caught on that particular stretch of the Thames. A few years ago, fishing without a specific target species using ground bait and maggots, I caught a 16 lb mirror carp from that stretch of river followed by Frank catching a 20 lb common carp, from the same spot, a few hours later.

Fifty years ago, I am not sure we could have caught a fish of that size and power under any circumstances with the tackle we were using. The mystery of what lived below the surface of that stretch of river fuelled the endless speculation and stories about these river monsters in our pub conversations for many years.

There were times when I would have preferred a better mode of transport to get me to my fishing destinations, but I would have to wait until next year, my 16th birthday, before my mode of transport would become motorised. Until then I was to be reliant on my trusty 3-speed Raleigh bicycle with modified panniers for the extra fishing luggage. I was loaded down with food, drinks and bait, but even so the journey to my fishing venues was seemingly effortless and rapid. I was athletically fit and strong, and it is amazing what anticipation, expectation and excitement can do for your energy levels. However, the opposite was also true when after a night's fishing the return trip home turned into a protracted slog. We were obviously tired from staying awake most of the night, but it was thoughts of school next day and possible homework to complete that made the journey a nightmare. Looking forward to a pint and pie at the Roebuck helped lift our mood a wee bit. Most of our fishing trips were at weekends during both school term time and school holidays. Most holidays, I would have committed weekdays and Saturdays to the hard work of landscape gardening or labouring. Although girlfriends and the odd family duty added to my time pressures, there was always a great sense of living life to the full. Work hard and play hard.

My fishing in 1965 was not confined to the Thames. The river Loddon was becoming our training ground for hemp seed and elderberry fishing. The time of year for hemp fishing is August to October – when the elderberries turn purple/black, and the theory goes, fall from the overhanging bushes into the awaiting fish mouths. Elderberries were used as hook bait with cooked hemp as feed/ground bait. The hook size was tiny (18 or 20) and the target fish, my river favourites – the beautiful roach and dace. Hemp is from the cannabis plant, and sure enough, once the fish had sensed and tasted the cooked hemp, they were literally hooked. Although the bait is tiny, the average fish size caught would usually be larger than would be expected with baits such as maggots. On a good day, or should I say a great day, I would catch over a hundred prime roach, dace and the occasional rudd. Despite the shoal being predated by pike and perch, the fish would continue to feed. The power of addiction, I suppose.

Norway 1965

This was to be a family trip to see my Norwegian relatives. My parents, two sisters and yours truly travelled by boat from Harwich to Kristiansand, an overnight crossing. My father's trusty Austin A30 enabled us to travel independently.

Accommodation constraints meant that, to my great delight, I was billeted to my uncle Halvar's *hytte* [summer house] and left to my own devices. It was situated in a superb position, close to the sea and the fishing boats. Although the summer house had electricity, the toilet was in a small shed in the garden, where a hole in a plank of wood led to a large bucket which quickly filled. At that time of year, the smell and hum from flying insects was an experience.

For reasons unknown to me, I hardly saw the rest of my English family. They were seeing the very large Norwegian contingent. My father had eleven brothers and sisters. There were the occasional large family get-togethers at Bestemor's house, which was within walking distance of my *hytte*, which I duly attended and enjoyed. Overall, this arrangement spared me from being endlessly stuffed full of food at each family's get together. Like the Jewish and Cornish, (as my Cornish wife would agree) the Norwegians are exceedingly generous hosts.

Having returned to my stomping grounds of five years previously, I was determined to enjoy the Norwegian countryside, sea scape, wildlife, and of course, the fishing. Now that my uncles and cousins had become my fishing buddies, there were regular trips out into the fjord. Barbecued whiting, cod and mackerel that were swimming in the fjord less than hour beforehand were tasting experiences to be remembered. I even became expert at frying these fish in butter on a stove inside Halvar's summer house. A long walk away was a stream that fed the same fjord, from which I managed to catch a few sea trout.

The abundance and availability of edible fresh fish means that Norwegians have a very different palate to that of the average UK resident. One day, I had just caught a perch of about 1 lb in weight in Farris Water, a freshwater lake near Larvik. Perch are very bony and even today, I would return them to the water if I was hungry. As I was admiring my catch, a Norwegian angler asked me if I would swap my very average perch for his beautiful 2 lb brown trout. After placing the trout in my bag, I asked what this guy was going to do with the perch. He explained that although there were more bones than meat, he was still going to eat it, apparently for its unique taste. Methinks I had the better part of the exchange.

Across the fjord from Halvar's *hytte* are two white sandy beaches suitable for swimming and sunbathing. With a relative rarity of soft sandy beaches around the coast of Norway, Nalum has always been a popular holiday venue. These beaches were a must to visit on sunny days. Although a long walk, my reward was to find the beach frequented with lovely young Scandinavian ladies. Just a few words in English would be a great way of introducing myself. Most encounters were very pleasant but didn't extend beyond the beach. I was beginning to believe that my likely chances of finding a girl to date was getting decidedly slim. However, following a pleasant chat with two extremely good-looking mature girls, a proposal of mine was accepted. I had mentioned that a friend of mine was joining me from England and possibly a foursome could be arranged. It was suggested by the girls to meet at the Grand Hotel, in Larvik on a certain time and date.

I had recently befriended Peter, who was a few years older than me, a great jive dancer who drove a red Reliant Robin (the same three-wheeler as Del Boy). He only needed a motorbike license to drive what he hoped would be his passion wagon. As far as I could see, Peter's entire focus in life was to meet girls. I had agreed that he could join me for a few days of my Norway adventure.

He was completely taken aback on his arrival when I announced that we were out that evening on a date. While we were waiting outside the Grand Hotel, Peter started to ridicule me, and suggested that the girls were a figment of my imagination. After about 10 minutes, even I was expecting a no-show. Then a brand-new black Mercedes saloon stopped in front of us and we were told to hop in. The expression on our faces must have been a sight to behold: I barely recognised the scantily clad girls from the beach as they were now dressed for a ball. Having regained his senses, Peter whispered that we were casually dressed, with only enough cash to buy a few pints of Pils lager. Even that was very expensive compared with English prices. It very quickly dawned on us that these girls were completely out of our league, but we decided to see how the evening would work out. They spoke very good English and suggested we visit a night club in Sandefjord, a town about 10 miles away.

When we arrived at the night club, it was part of an expensive hotel. Our fears were realised when there was a valet service to park the car. At the entrance of the nightclub, I had what I believe was a stroke of genius. I suggested that the girls enter the club while Peter and I would go to the hotel foyer to cash some of our English pounds for Norwegian krone. Instead, we briskly walked out and eventually managed to hitch-hike back to Nalum.

Our next adventure was a disco/dance in a large school hall in Larvik. As the dance floor was part of a newly refurbished gymnasium all attendees had to remove their shoes and leave them in the changing rooms. The dance was very enjoyable. I noticed that every time 'Cadillac' by the Hep Stars was played, the dance floor erupted. Chatting to some girls, Peter and I were one of the last to collect our shoes. Mine were missing. My unique purple suede winkle-picker shoes, my pride and joy – nicked. Someone had taken a fancy to them and left me his own black leather shoes. I knew that these had to belong to the scumbag because they also fitted me very well. For the rest of my time in Norway, I would keep looking at men's footwear with the vague hope of spotting them.

I still miss those unique shoes today!

For some obscure reason Peter and I decided then to travel to Denmark, via the ferry from Larvik to Frederikshavn. As we had little money for a hotel, our evening ended up being spent in the cell of a Danish prison, having been arrested for being homeless vagrants. Once released we spent the day on the town beach. For me the high spot of the trip, was meeting a lovely girl called Liv-May, who I then arranged to meet back in Norway after she invited me, without Peter, to a party.

My philosophy of the mid '60s could be summarised by the words of Junior Walker and the All Stars song – 'Road Runner'.

> 'Love the Life I Live'
> 'Live the Life I Love'

Brian Halvorsen: The teenager of the week

A BRACKNELL schoolboy recently gained his first county honour when he played for the Berkshire under-15 rugby team against Oxfordshire. He is Brian Halvorsen, of 3, Furzemoors, Bracknell—our teenager of the week. Brian, who has been playing rugby for four years, played as a winger for the Berkshire team. He contributed three points (from a try) to his side's 14—3 victory.

He is a pupil at Ranelagh School. It was here he first started to play rugby four years ago. Now he is captain of the school's under-15 team and also plays in the first team.

Before the school broke up for the Christmas holiday, Brian was presented with his rugby colours.

Last summer he was a member of the Berkshire under-15 athletics team. He gained a gold badge in the final of the south-east Berkshire athletics competition.

Most of his spare time is devoted to sport—cricket, basketball, gymnastics, as well as rugby. For the past two years he has been a member of Bracknell Athletic Club.

"Most boys who play rugby at school like the game," said Brian. "But a lot of them forget about it when they leave. Only the keen ones keep at it. I hope to keep on playing after I leave school.

INSTEAD OF "PUNCH-UPS"

"I like playing sport. Besides being great fun it helps me to let out some of my energy, instead of having punch-ups."

His hobbies include fishing and bird watching. Brian is a member of a pop group called "Grimble"—the other three members are also pupils of Ranelagh School.

"We are making good progress with the group even though we don't have much time for rehearsal. But we're not in a great hurry to go places—we just enjoy playing because it's fun.

"I think the national pop scene is changing at the moment. A little while ago it was very exciting, but now it has quietened down. I think it will liven up soon enough."

Brian hopes to study physics and chemistry at "A" level and perhaps work at Harwell Atomic Energy Station. He would like to do research in nuclear physics.

His other ambition is to travel around the world. Last year he visited Norway and Denmark, and this year he will be travelling to France.

Teenager of the Week

BRIAN HALVORSEN, of 3, Furzemoors, Bracknell—teenager of the week.

There's one thing to look back and say 'Those were the good old days', but it's another to realise that I was living and feeling every moment of this fantastic period of my life.

Although I thoroughly enjoyed my trip to Norway, I was itching to get back to time on the riverbank. Even the thought of attending school was no big downer as I would re-establish the tightening bonds with all my associated friends, and to continue with my sporting activities.

I was chosen as Teenager of the Week by the local newspaper, *Bracknell News*, after scoring a try playing for Berkshire against Oxfordshire. Rugby was becoming my main sport, and if I wasn't playing for the school, I would be part of either Bracknell Colts or the Senior Bracknell 1st team.

With all my social and sporting activities, I had two often repeated remarks from my mother: 'Oh no, not more dirty kit to wash' and 'You treat our home like a hotel'. Looking back, my home environment was loving and caring, and my parents were very easy going and liberal. On one occasion my mother came home to catch me listening to records and canoodling with a girl on the sofa. After the embarrassed girlfriend had left the house, my mother's comment was: 'I wish you would have let me know, the house is not looking its best'. I am grateful that my parents were both tolerant and pragmatic.

Bear's Christmas party

In September, Bear told me that sadly his mother had passed away after a short illness. We would often walk to school together and as far as I could gather, he seemed to be coping reasonably well. Just before we broke up for Christmas holidays, Bear announced he was staging an open house party starting on 23 December. I was taken aback when he announced that his father and his new girlfriend were going away on holiday and leaving him alone in the family home over Christmas with nothing but a shed load of cash to buy his own presents and food.

The main party was set for Christmas Eve, but friends were invited to use the facilities as soon as Bear's father and girlfriend had departed. Many of my school friends turned up – any excuse for a good party!

Christmas Eve, the house was packed out with uninvited party revellers, drugs, drink and smoke – it was pandemonium. I had invited a girl who was older than me and had her own car! I was hoping for some action but because of the sheer chaos I quickly realised that this was a nonstarter. After about an hour we began to get concerned by some of the guests who had taken up residence in the bedrooms and were raiding the house for food and drugs. As the drugs were from the medicine cabinet, I dread to think what they were taking. The situation was out of control, so we suggested to Bear to come home with us and possibly return next morning. He appeared to be unconcerned by the chaos and was happy to stay. Later Bear informed us that concerned neighbours had called the police, who eventually cleared the house and helped reassemble some of the furniture.

Christmas morning Frank, Jim, the Daves and I returned to the scene of the previous night's mayhem, bearing a small turkey and the trimmings for Bear's Christmas lunch. The scene that met us was concerning. Furniture that was beyond repair was piled in the front garden with countless beer cans, piles of food packaging and all sorts of suspicious deposits. As we approached the front door there was several patches of pavement pizza. Surprisingly when Bear opened the door, he seemed unconcerned about the state of the place. We offered to help him tidy things up, but he said that it would be his father's problem, as he was off to stay with his aunt for the rest of the holidays.

Bear was very grateful for the turkey and decided to cook it the moment we had cleared the cooker of piles of cigarette ash, butt ends and broken glass. While we all were trying to make the kitchen habitable, Bear turned the gas oven on but in his dazed state forgot to light it. In the meantime, we decided to take a tour of the remainder of the house and inspect the damage. When we returned to the kitchen, Bear realised the turkey wasn't cooking, so he opened the oven and lit a match.

Boom!

He was blasted onto the kitchen table which was still piled full of fag ends, ash, beer cans and stale beer. We couldn't help to see the funny side of seeing Bear spreadeagled across the table with hair on end, eyebrows scorched, and a puzzled dazed expression. To complete the picture, he was covered in lumps of raw turkey, sage and onion stuffing and fag ash. The destruction of the entire kitchen was now virtually complete.

After taking stock of the situation, Bear finally relented and accepted my invitation to have Christmas lunch with my family.

You could say that 1965 ended with a bang.

1966

The year started cold and cheerless, but a few successful fishing trips to our favourite rivers brought my life view back into perspective. My anticipation of a great year to come was already being realised.

For several of the fishing trips before term started on 8 January, the temperature would not go above zero. On reeling in our fishing lines, the water would freeze and jam the line flow at the rod tip. Did this put us off? Not at all. Flasks of tea and coffee, hand warmers, and layers of thermals meant that we were snug as a bug in a rug. Just being on the riverbank, catching fish and listening to my new transistor radio, a Christmas present, made our trips worthwhile. Besides Frank, Richard was a regular fishing buddy and so too, occasionally, was Bear. There was always a competitive banter between us. From the moment we parked our bikes, there was a frenzied dash for the best swim. This would continue with who's caught the most and/or the biggest and telling little white lies about what bait combination or size of hook was proving successful.

On one occasion, Frank and I began to compete against each other, without acknowledging as much. When my groundbait ran out, Frank refused to lend me anymore. Without a constant introduction of fresh fish food, my flow of bites would and did dry up. However, my aggravation did not end there. The stretch of river flowed over 6 feet deep close to the bank. Not content with trying to prevent me catching any more fish, Frank decided to lift my keep net out of the water to count and check the size of my catch. A few moments later, unseen by me, Frank had slipped on the wet grass into the river. On hearing a gentle splash, I turned to where he had been mucking around to see nothing but his hat! The river, being so fast and deep had carried him, completely submerged, past me. He was a very good swimmer, so I was confident that Frank would eventually turn up. Sure enough, he did – and despite being soaking wet, he then poured some more ground bait into my bucket. I thanked him for his generosity and in return gave him a cup of tea from my flask. On looking to where Frank had been fishing and seeing his hat sitting on the bank without its owner, we both creased up laughing.

Over 50 years later, the recurring atmosphere with my fishing buddies – no matter whom I am fishing with – is laughing at our various misfortunes nearly always accompanied with a friendly but competitive edge.

Is it me, or does this occur among most of the angling fraternity?

The eel

In February, Richard and I revisited our pike fishing spot at Virginia Water. We had several bites, but none enabled us to put a fish on the bank. Richard caught a nice perch, while I decided to try a different part of the bay. No sooner had the float settled than it slowly slid underwater. Waiting a minute before striking, and even using heavy pike tackle, I quickly realised that this was no ordinary fish. In fact, it was a specimen freshwater eel, weighing over 4 lb. It was and still is, the largest eel that I have ever caught. Eels are virtually all muscle, and this monster was no exception. It fought like a fish five times heavier. We were alarmed by the sight of a stainless-steel gaff being bent out of shape by this creature wrapping its muscular body around and distorting the metal shank.

Richard was obsessed with wanting to eat the thing. Many hours later in my parent's kitchen, I chopped off the eel's head. Richard had the fright of his life when he decided to mess around with the fish's head. On placing his finger inside the eel's mouth, it immediately clamped its teeth hard down on his finger. It was a macabre scene, Richard walking towards me waving a huge eel's head attached to his finger. After extricating his digit and still being in a state of shock, he decided not to eat the freshly fried body of this creature that, even dead, was intent on making Richard the meal.

Richard with the menacing eel

Love of history

One of my favourite subjects at school was History. I have always had an open and inquiring mind about the past, and my interest was awakened when I was told that history was a subject that told His Story – Man's Story. Just learning the facts and dates was no longer good enough. I wanted to know the whys and wherefores, especially the background behind the significant events in history. I was lucky to have an excellent teacher.

In one of his lessons, we were asked to discuss the likely causes of the French Revolution. He asked the thought-provoking question: *Why would you revolt and take up arms against your own government?*

All sorts of answers were proffered: didn't like the king, unfair society, bad laws, too many taxes, etc. Our teacher discussed them all, and kept asking if these factors were really bad enough to risk your life and openly revolt against your own government. After much debate we agreed that these sets of circumstances didn't warrant taking part and risking one's life in a civil war. He then described the dire situation in France at that time. Large sectors of the population were starving. The teacher then asked if we would stand by and watch our children die from starvation and disease when the ruling classes appeared not to care and the queen suggested eating cake as a solution to the lack of essentials such as bread.

To my mind this was inspired, thought-provoking education. With the huge divisions in our society today, could something similar occur?

It was about this time that I started having real doubts about the truthfulness of the news. It didn't seem to matter if the media was television, radio, newspapers or magazines. The USA were pouring troops into Vietnam and bombing the hell out of the Northern Vietnamese in the name of stopping the spread of Communism. Great protest songs and huge anti-war rallies all over the world were telling a different story, or at least a different point of view. Britain, USA, France and Russia were all letting off atomic bombs into the atmosphere – and the media was treating this as normal.

The USA spent months recovering four hydrogen bombs that they lost over Spain following the crash of a B52 bomber. One of the bombs that was recovered from the Mediterranean Sea was 70 megaton – 5,000 times more powerful than the atomic bomb that levelled Hiroshima but I wasn't aware of this at the time as media coverage was scant. There is still some radiation around Palomares today!

Harold Wilson was re-elected as Prime Minister. The year previously he had awarded the Beatles MBE's which illustrated a more progressive approach to younger celebrities.

The *big* event of 1966 has to be the World Cup. For me, I was overjoyed for the team, but still preferred to spend my time on the riverbank rather than go out celebrating. For England, it was not only a time of euphoria and celebrations with England beating Germany 4–2 in extra time, but a well needed restoration of national pride. We, as a country, could now claim that Britain was a nation of sporting success as well as pop groups and fashion.

The plight of the Welsh mining communities was brought into sharp focus by the Aberfan Disaster. On 21 October, we as a country were shocked by the horrendous loss of life in this small community. One hundred and sixteen children and twenty-eight adults killed by a preventable landslide in South Wales. Again, most people can reflect back to what they were doing when the news broke of that disaster.

As the year progressed the news that was regularly and repeatedly reported in the UK media was that of USA's space missions, anti-war/nuclear weapons protests, the escalation of the Vietnam war, and ever larger nuclear tests. For me the defeating of Henry Cooper by Cassius Clay (twice) was more notable, and of much greater relevance to me as a regular pub-goer was the introduction of tougher new drink driving laws.

Making arrangements such as meeting girlfriends was difficult, especially if they lived beyond cycling distance. Virtually everybody I knew at that time didn't have a home phone. My nearest communication centre was fifty yards from home, a classic red public telephone box. As my social life was spreading beyond Bracknell, I could often be seen standing outside the red box armed with coins – it was a pay as you go system with an initial cost of two pennies. There was also the added uncertainty of waiting for an incoming call, hoping that nobody else was on the line. Can you imagine giving your latest girlfriend the number of a public call box as your contact number?

The other major form of communication was the letter, often a convenient way of calling off a relationship. I had a few 'Dear John' letters. 'Dear Brian, sorry to stand you up but my cat died'. 'Sorry I can't make next Saturday, but I just realised that's the evening I wash my hair.' At least they bothered to write.

* * *

Some of my favourite songs that related to letters and the post:

'Dear John' – Skeeter Davis & Bobby Bare

'Return To Sender' – Elvis Presley

'Please Mr Postman' – The Marvelettes and the Beatles

'P.S. I Love You' – The Beatles

'Love Letters' – Ketty Lester

'The Letter' – Box Tops

'Roll Over Beethoven' – Chuck Berry

'I'm Gonna Sit Right Down and Write Myself a Letter' – Paul McCartney, Bill Haley and His Comets, *et al.*

Before the age of mobile phones and texts these songs did have a significance for many of us in the context of romantic trials and tribulations. A letter from a girl who was a few years older than me and was attending boarding school, was opened by mistake by my parents. Although I was embarrassed, the letter did spark a conversation with my Mum. It became clear to me that I had a limited knowledge of intimate relationships and my parents were not forthcoming with information. Believing the subject matter was too embarrassing for them, I felt it wasn't my place to pursue the subject.

At this time, I was going through the usual uncertainties and self-doubt that comes with starting meaningful relationships.

After meeting at a village dance, I was invited to spend a Sunday with the family of a very attractive new girlfriend. Unbeknown to me, her younger brother was a junior Go-Kart champion and the morning was spent at Blackbushe Airport watching him win some exciting races. On returning to the girl's home, I was offered a cup of tea by her very welcoming mother. For some bizarre reason the conversation turned to debating what comes first, the tea or the milk. Her mother and I agreed that the milk came first – girlfriend disagreed. In an unexpected turn of events and before I could say 'More tea, vicar', I was told in no uncertain terms to leave! Lovely family; nutcase girlfriend.

On reflection, I realised that there was still much to learn!

As my personal development was changing rapidly, the music of 1966 seemed to becoming more relevant and poignant to my deepest emotions, especially the classic love songs.

The Beatles and Stones were both capitalising on their fame and popularity of the previous year, releasing fantastic albums and singles.

Fed by the mainstream media, the strong impression that most of us believed to be true was that the Beatles were clean-cut, clean living and their music popularised mainstream, whereas the Rolling Stones were diametrically opposite. It appears that this wasn't entirely accurate. Members of both groups were good friends, socialised together and even shared ideas musically. Drugs were used by both groups, but it appears that the Stones were the group that courted negative publicity and had various scrapes with the authorities.

Rolling Stones

'Out Of Time' – also a giant hit for Chris Farlowe

'Mother's Little Helper'

'Under My Thumb'

'Stupid Girl'

Released singles.

'Paint It Black'

'Nineteenth Nervous Breakdown'

'Have You Seen Your Mother Baby Standing in The Shadows'

To me, the lyrics of these songs were raw, misogynistic and also reflected some dark sides of society.

Beatles

Revolver Album. Started a new era for the Beatles with tracks like:

'Tomorrow Never Knows' (drugs/psychedelic leaning)

'Taxman' (a protest song about the 95% tax on unearned income in the UK)

'Yellow Submarine'/ 'Eleanor Rigby' (loneliness/futility)

'Nowhere Man' and 'Yesterday' are some of my all-time meaningful songs.

'Day Tripper/ 'We Can Work It Out' and 'Paperback Writer' were also released as singles. The Beatles were starting to lose their fresh-faced witty image, especially John Lennon.

The 'Others'

Point of interest – did David Jones change his last name to Bowie to avoid being confused with Davy Jones of the Monkees 'I'm A Believer' fame?

The Beach Boys

Pet Sounds album. Great tracks/ singles from the album 'God Only Knows'; 'Good Vibrations'; 'Sloop John B' and 'Caroline No'.

Spencer Davis Group

Three great singles in 1966. 'Keep On Running', 'Somebody Help Me' and 'Gimme Some Loving'. Steve Winwood – what a rock voice.

The Kinks

'Sunny Afternoon'. No. 1 when England won the World Cup (July) and the song was part of the euphoria and atmosphere that gripped England. However, 'Sunny Afternoon' was another pop song complaining about the UK tax system. 'Dead End Street'; 'Dedicated Follower of Fashion', and 'Til The End Of The Day' were all classics in 1966.

The Troggs

Great singles – 'Wild Thing', 'Any Way That You Want Me', 'With A Girl Like You' and the naughty 'I Can't Control Myself' banned by the BBC in the UK and in Australia.

Jimmy Hendrix

'Hey Joe'. One of the greatest guitarists, great classic psychedelic record.

The Who

'Substitute'. Resonated with me.

Small Faces

'All or Nothing'. Sung with such feeling by Steve Marriott.

Otis Redding

'My Girl'. Absolute classic and great to smooch to.

Jimmy Ruffin

'What Becomes of The Broken Hearted'. Another classic- such a sad soulful love song.

Percy Sledge

'When a Man Loves a Woman'. The ultimate unconditional love song. Only Percy can sing this song.

Mick, a nearby friend and a bit of a Rocker, who introduced me to R&B /Blues/ Rock gave me a greater understanding of the origins of modern pop culture. Listening to the likes of John Mayall, Muddy Water's, Sonny Boy Williamson, Howlin' Wolf, John Lee Hooker, etc. who were some of the early blues greats, who led me on a further voyage of discovery which in turn led me to:

Cream

With the legendary guitarist and singer Eric Clapton, singer and bassist Jack Bruce, and drummer Ginger Baker. Cream is widely regarded as the world's first 'supergroup'.

Album – *Fresh Cream* with tracks 'NSU' and 'I'm So Glad'.

Dusty Springfield

Like many others I regard her as one of Britain's greatest blues singers. 'Goin' Back' – although I enjoyed this great song at the time, it was many years later that the words became so relevant and significant.

> 'Let everyone debate the true reality
> I'd rather see the world the way it used to be'

* * *

During the tail end of the summer holidays, Frank and I organised a combined camping and fishing trip to a lake near Reading. Earlier forays both to the lake and the River Kennet flowing nearby showed signs of promise, especially for big tench and perch. The plan was to fish the river by day and the lake, adjacent to our tent, by night.

Using maggots and hempseed, both of us were catching lovely prime roach and dace. Fishing the lake on the first evening, we experienced a distinct lack of bites, so after brewing a cup tea on our trusty Primus stove, we decided on a good night's sleep inside the tent. In the morning, I decided to leave my match rod with very fine line and small hook dangling at the lakeside while frying up eggs and bacon for breakfast. Frank casually suggested that I should pick my rod up, as it was heading into the lake.

On picking the rod up, the fish was determined to keep going. Having a very weak line, I had very little alternative but to let more line out. There was a small problem, however: no more line to let out. Determined not to lose the fish, I decided to walk into the lake, keeping contact with the unseen monster fish. The walk turned into a swim with rod in one hand and swimming with the other. Suddenly the fish had enough of playing with me and powered off at high speed, not only snapping my line but also taking all that was left on the reel. Another one that got away!

That night we decided to fish a small weir pool using as bait some raw bacon, left over from breakfast. Leaving the lines in the water, we slept through most of the night. It was with some degree of surprise that in the morning, both our rods had hooked a barbel. Although these were small, they were the first we had seen, let alone caught at this venue. A nice finish to our memorable trip.

With all the camping gear, as well as the fishing gear, we were grateful for transportation by our parents, especially when it was time to pack up and return home. Asked about our trip, we told our parents that the fishing was great and the overall experience eventful.

* * *

September was when I was becoming excited about having my first motorised form of transport. I had a very limited budget, so it was fortunate that a friend of my parents had a motor bike/scooter for sale: a BSA Sunbeam 175 scooter, priced £18. I, like most people, had never heard of this model, but in my situation, beggars can't be choosers. Although the superstructure was shaped similarly to scooters such as the more popular Lambretta and Vespas, the mechanics were taken from the motorcycles that were being manufactured by Sunbeam at that time. I was not particularly bothered that the scooter wasn't the most trendy of models because having a motorised means of getting about would change every aspect of my life. Apparently, that particular model is so rare that it is now worth a lot of money.

I passed my driving test within days of buying the scooter. This meant that I could transport my friends and myself to fishing venues in a fraction of the time and effort. No longer reliant on public transport or lifts from my older friends, I could now travel to visit girls and clubs outside of Bracknell and district. When it was inconvenient to walk to school, I would park the Sunbeam near the rear entrance of my school. In 1966 my running costs were relatively low, even allowing for years of inflation. Driving License – 5 shillings (25p); a gallon (5 litres) of petrol – 5 shillings. With an expanding social life and to maintain my new lifestyle, working at weekends and school holidays would now become a priority. Financial assistance from my parents was zero.

My confidence and self-image with the opposite sex was now improving. I started a relationship with a girl from my year group after having a passionate encounter with her at a rather good school party. She was from an entirely different social class. Her parents lived in a posh Victorian house in Ascot and had the use of a private box at the racecourse. She spoke with a lovely soft plummy voice and appeared to be comfortable with my working-class attitudes. Her interests were completely different to mine: she loved classical music, played the violin, and tennis.

On one occasion, close to her home in Ascot, she volunteered me to help out at a high-class jumble sale. On sorting through the clothes, I came across a full-length purple rabbit fur coat. It was super soft and in very good condition. For me it was love at first sight. Being a helper, I managed to negotiate a price of two shillings (10 p) for what would be my pride and joy for the next few years. As soon as I arrived home, the fur coat was shortened to a length that made it more suited for sitting on my scooter. I was aware that the basic requirements to be recognised as a Mod were to have a scooter and a parka, preferably with a big faux fur collar. I did not want to be labelled a full-blown Mod, but having a scooter, a fur coat and a short haircut gave me something of the right image – I was a half-baked Mod. My dilemma was that many of my older friends were Rockers and I had much in common with their principles, values and music.

To complete my unique fashion statement, my father allowed me to wear his Norwegian cap – high at the front, big peak and a flap to cover my neck and ears, the sort that Russian peasants would wear especially in winter. Together with a pair of sunglasses, I was considered a real trendy geezer – or a complete motorised numpty.

What about crash helmets? Never gave them a thought until the wearing of them was made compulsory in 1973, by which time I was motoring on four wheels.

This was a time when the younger generation were taking part in ant-war protests but also love and peace movements. The mainstream media tried to discredit this movement by epitomising the long-haired hippies who were labelled as the counterculture. For me in Bracknell, it was a rarity to encounter a peace-loving, free-love hippy type. That would come later. What was relevant to my social environment and would show itself at dances and parties was the local wars between Mods and Rockers.

The hostilities between them would often erupt into viscous fights. These would often break out spontaneously with knives, spanners and bicycle chains all being part of the weaponry. On these occasions my group of friends would stay well clear of trouble, and had befriended three of the biggest, ugliest and vicious rockers you could imagine, who declared: 'Anyone gives you lads trouble and they'll have us to deal with' in a broad Berkshire accent. Although we had this protection, a hasty exit was our normal course of action, before the police arrived with their 'Hurry Up wagons' – so called because they were used for mass arrests.

Having a scooter and fur coat placed me in the Mod camp. This could be problematic when running into a pack of hairy bikers at a roadside café. There was no way my 175cc Sunbeam could outrun a 650cc Norton. Fortunately, a brief explanation of my views, especially when mentioning a shared love of Rock and Blues music, quickly settled matters and new friendships and alliances were made. I was genuinely neutral over my allegiances. However, when questioned by one side or the other, neutrality wasn't an option. I tried not to get involved in punch-ups.

I did have a pugnacious side of me, especially being fit, active, and with an overload of hormones. My release was to channel this pent-up aggression by playing competitive sport, especially rugby. I am always reminded of the quotation '*Rugby is a hooligan's game played by gentlemen; football is a gentleman's game played by hooligans*'.

Returning to school, for Michaelmas term, was a sharp reminder that next year was exam year for me and my year group. It was made clear that the school's expectations in the forthcoming exams were high. Ranelagh was a grammar school with a longstanding reputation for very high academic standards. Although I was in the A stream, my grades were slipping, which led to an interview with the headmaster, the 'Beak'. Being that I was a key sportsman and captain of most of the school teams of my year, he was concerned about my future at the school. The Beak (who actually did have a large, curved hooter), enquired about possible reasons for my poor homework and asked if anything be done to improve the situation. I was very aware that were it not for my being a sporting asset to the school, the interview might have ended in six of the best with the feared cane.

The most likely reason for my poor academic showing was primarily due to my enjoying a busy lifestyle outside of school activities and a general antipathy for many of the subjects on the curriculum. Trying to find a suitable excuse, I described that the conditions at home were not ideal for home studying. There was an element of truth to this because I carried out my written work in our family's busy dining room.

Next day my parents were summoned to the headmaster's study, the upshot being that my father had to construct a desk in my bedroom. This was the first time my parents had any face-to-face contact with anybody from my school, and the impact on them was tangible. Desk built, I was banished to my room until all homework was duly completed. As I was taking eight GCE subjects the homework by my standards, was often difficult and relentless. My excuse now eliminated, the only sensible way forward was to knuckle down and do the work.

During the Michaelmas term, most of my friends who attended grammar schools and who were in a similar situation to myself, started preparing themselves for the mock exams. Many curtailed their weekday social activities for exam revision. In addition to the extra workload both in school and at home, many of our teachers encouraged us to answer past exam papers which they freely supplied. To my way of thinking this would give us the edge, but was a little bit like cheating. Being ambivalent about the relevance of these exams, I decided to do no more than was strictly necessary. I remember thinking that my estate mates who attended the secondary modern school appeared to have far less pressure placed upon them, and were given less complicated and lengthy homework. As the actual exams were many months into the future, my mates who attended the local secondary school hadn't considered starting any revision. I was beginning to see that the early opportunities in life, especially in education, were not always on a level playing field. Over fifty years later, nothing appears to have changed that much.

Despite the nearness of the important mock exams, many after-school activities such as rugby, hockey, gymnastic competitions and basketball matches continued as normal. I still attended the youth club, but night clubs, pubs and dances were reserved for Friday and Saturdays. I made every effort to keep Sundays as my fishing day. All freshwater angling for course fish was halted by the close season. Unlike today, the close season for coarse fishing extended to all lakes and rivers, so there was an enforced break. It would end on 16 June, by which time all of my GCE papers would have finished. Although

I didn't enjoy this period of deprivation, I reluctantly accepted the situation. In hindsight, I realised that it did give me a better chance of preparing for the exam onslaught of 1967.

A weekend to remember

On the eve of 17 June, we arrived at the River Loddon just before dark to set up for the night. Even in summer the river runs deep and fast, so ledgering with bunches of maggots or worms with bucket loads of groundbait was our method of attack. It wasn't long before my keepnet was crowded with prime roach, dace, perch and small chub. It was pitch-black and my method of detecting bites was by shining a torch onto my rod tip.

A solid pull of the rod, and very quickly came the realisation that this was a completely different class of fish. This was confirmed by shining the torchlight on the fish as it approached the bank. I shouted for Frank to help me land a beautiful 5 lb barbel. Not a monster by Loddon standards, but for me a specimen to cherish. Once my heart stopped pounding, I just sat with a huge smile marvelling at my achievement. The rest of the night brought more fish, including bream and perch, but catching my first decent sized barbel had made this trip special.

Having agreed to work next day for Engel and after enjoying a couple of hours of early morning fishing, I packed up my fishing gear and cycled the 12 miles home. After making myself scrambled eggs on toast and a cup of tea, I was ready for work by 7.30 a.m. The day's workload mainly involved weeding an enormous flower bed. This would normally be a complete bore, but the actions of the previous night kept me unusually content. The music playing on my radio also contributed to sustaining the smile on my face.

That evening, at a school party, instead of feeling knackered and bored after having fished all night, the opposite was true. I was verging on hyperactive and in a state of euphoria. I put it down to the afterglow of a great fishing trip, a good day's work gardening, lovely sunny warm weather and the company of good friends. The atmosphere of the party was magical, aided by great music such as 'Paint it Black' (Rolling Stones), 'A Groovy Kind of Love' (The Mindbenders), 'When a Man Loves a Woman' (Percy Sledge), 'Wild Thing' (The

Troggs) and many more. Another mood enhancer may have been that the rooms of the party were thick with the smoke of pot.

The weekend was completed with a visit to the Red Lion, where a few pints of beer with the local lads, was kindly paid for by the generosity of Frank's father. Because all pubs closed at 2 p.m. on Sunday, I had lunch at home with the family, a rare occasion and a time to catch up with them. All in all, the weekend was truly memorable. With the completion of end of term exams and the end of most formal lessons, even the thought of attending school next morning wasn't too bad.

Later that summer, Richard and I decided on an all-night fishing session on the mainstream of the Thames at Shiplake. It was a lovely sunny August day and as the holiday boat traffic diminished, the still evening brought perfect fishing conditions. The fishing was enjoyable with both of us catching plenty of nice bream, roach and dace. As darkness descended, the temperature rapidly dropped, making us glad we had our winter coats and flasks of hot tea and coffee. However, the peace and quiet of the night were shattered by loud disco music blaring out from a posh house on the opposite side of the river. Although the noise from the party wasn't affecting the fishing, I was feeling a tinge of envy as the partygoers appeared to be having a rip-roaring time.

About 1 a.m. we could hear a faint slopping sound close to my swim. Could this be a mega carp basking close to the bank? Because it was very dark, I shone my powerful torch in the direction of the splashing. To my surprise, the beam of light focused on a man's shrunken anatomy. Standing next to him was a buck-naked nubile girl. Both appeared comfortable in the spotlight. Although I couldn't take my eyes off this bizarre scene, a drunken slurring voice asked if we had caught many fish. I retorted that it had been going well, but we were now concerned that on casting out our weights, we might hook more than fish, shining the torch back on the male swimmer's block and tackle. They wished us a good night and swam back to the party. Richard and I were nonplussed. Despite the cold, we continued fishing, both of us hooking what we labelled 'boats' – huge fish that swam off, snapping our lines with their power.

On another night-time outing that summer, our fishing was disturbed by loud raunchy music coming from a brightly lit commercial pleasure boat that was heading upstream. From the commentary and general commotion, we realised that the partygoers were inebriated women being entertained by two male strippers. After about an hour, the boat was on its downstream return, with all the lights on, but the music had stopped. To our surprise and amusement, we could clearly see two naked men being chased around the decks by a hoard of crazed women in all stages of undress. The strippers were clearly distressed and were genuinely screaming for help. The performers realised that they were trapped on board, and escape was impossible in the pitch black, midstream and surrounded by fast-flowing water. Hazards of the job!

For me, 1966 was a time of transition where it was becoming apparent that I had to take a more realistic look at where life was taking me. School and sport – especially rugby – needed more of my time and attention, which were not exactly hardships. However, the need to have a girlfriend was still uppermost in my mind! I realised that relationships with the opposite sex were far more complex than I imagined. The complications of forming meaningful relationships also led to both confusing and disturbing emotional problems to solve. The time spent fishing was also becoming a time when I could meditate and reflect. While sitting on the bank, I would often recite to myself: 'Lucky in love, unlucky at fishing and vice versa'. Looking back, I believe that sitting on the riverbank and enjoying being close to nature, was giving me some psychological and meditational space that I needed during a time of emotional turbulence and vulnerability.

Bracknell, like many expanding towns, was developed from a charming small single high street village into a 1960s town with a shopping centre with several department stores and numerous clothing and fashion shops. At the time these held little interest for my friends and me. However, the new Wimpy coffee bar did become the place to be; it was my first experience of café culture. When strapped for cash, a gang of us would buy a cup of coffee and make it last until we were asked to buy something else or leave.

During part of that summer holidays, I worked on a production line manufacturing new perfumes and cosmetics. Immediately after work, I would make haste for the café, hoping to meet the girl of my dreams. On one occasion, I couldn't help but notice that a group of girls kept looking and smiling at me. Full of bravado, I introduced myself and enquired about my obvious attraction to them. I was taken aback when they explained that it wasn't my looks that fascinated them, but my powerful perfumed smell. To keep the conversation going, I explained that the cause of my distinct aromas came from a perfume factory, and I gave them all some samples from work. I couldn't understand why they seemed a bit indignant. The product that I had purloined and was now offering these girls was Femfresh.

During the summer term, the main school sport was cricket. I was a distinctly average cricketer, whereas Richard was a fabulous bowler and played for Berkshire. Most inter-school matches were arranged for Saturdays and although being a low order batsman, I felt that the team wouldn't miss me – and that there were better things to do. For me, weekends were reserved for earning money and fishing. Also, I enjoyed other sports, such as athletics. I was for a few years the county shotput champion. Having won the county championship earlier that year, I was selected to compete in the South of England competition. I was surprised and confused when my sports teacher refused me permission to compete, saying that school cricket took priority.

Without any discussion with my games master and a weak excuse, I decided to abscond from the cricket match in favour of adding another shot putt title. My rationale was based on the assumption that the school's reputation would be better enhanced by me representing the school in the regional athletics.

Sitting on the coach on the way to the championships with my fellow athletes, I was surprised when our last stop was outside Reading Gaol. We were joined by four inmates, young offenders who were entered into the sprint events, on merit. They were dressed quite normally – no handcuffs, no stripes or arrows on their clothes, but all had short haircuts. Their behaviour was polite and friendly, surprisingly better than I would have expected from most people of my age group. In conversation, the question of why they had been locked up was revealed. Two of them for murder – yes, *murder* – and the other two for GBH. During all the time I spent with these guys, my overall impression was that they were respectful and considerate.

At the event, I had high hopes of winning the shot putt. Most of my competitors were much bigger than me in all directions, but mainly slow, obese and with poor technique. One guy however, had a similar style and speed to me, but was considerably taller and more athletic. Needless to say, he beat me into second place by a huge margin and went on to become the national champion with a new UK record.

The trip taught me a couple of important lessons. No matter how good you think you are, there's always someone better. The young criminals acquitted themselves well, especially in the relay race. None of the non-criminal element of our team were beaten up or murdered on the journey home. Once they had been dropped off to resume their sentences, we all agreed that it is important not to judge people only by their personal history and reputation.

Even my school sports master, Norman, didn't kick up too badly that I missed the cricket match.

Fine dining

One of my very local estate friends, Dave P, developed a passion for cooking and started work at the Manor, a newly opened Berni Inn at the top of Bracknell High Street. Although only 16 years old, Dave quickly became a part-time sous chef, while full time at his secondary school. Those early days in the professional kitchen proved to be the start of his very successful career in hotel management including at the RAC Club in the Mall and running a chain of major hotels in South Africa.

It was just before Christmas when Dave P booked a table for the estate lads in the restaurant, with the promise of large discounts. The evening started well, with a few pints of beer and the Berni Inn's unique tipple, Harvey's Bristol Cream. For most of us, this was our first fine dining experience – prawn cocktail followed by a fantastic steak. I just loved the whole experience. Dave was acting as mine host when the waitress serving his steak gave him the filthiest look, slamming his food down with a sneering tone of disgust and mimicking being sick. 'I suppose this is yours, P,' she said, with the emphasis on his surname. Except for Dave P, we all fell about laughing, and even today we refer to Dave by his surname with a disparaging tone, just to remind him of that occasion.

For my own part, this was the beginning of a passion for fine wines, fine dining, cafés, restaurants – and anywhere I can find good food and nowadays great coffee, funds allowing. Thereafter, during the '60s a meal at one of the Berni Inns would represent the pinnacle of fine dining and would be reserved for those important occasions and special girls. On reflection, if I had kept more of my leisure time to fishing, sports, low-cost dining and the occasional trip to the pub, my wealth might have been considerably enhanced. Do I have any regrets about these lifestyle habits developed from the '60s? Not one.

1967

A year in which decisions and events that would significantly influence my future was about to happen, many of these events I could not have predicted in my wildest dreams. For me and for most fifth-form pupils in full time education, especially in state schools, the major decision of that time was: 'Do I stay on at school, or do I get a job?'

At Ranelagh my options would be influenced and decided by my GCE exam results. My mock exam results were not great, except for history, chemistry and biology. I have always enjoyed the biological sciences, especially the subjects involving living creatures, including my fellow man. At that time, I had fairly fixed views: I was uninspired by plant life and anything to do with botany. Any subjects that I could envision being interesting and relevant for a career in the healing and caring professions became a priority. Beyond that, any prospects of a future in any profession were looking obscure to say the least.

Having an uncertain route going forward and with the backing of my parents, I applied for several jobs in and around Bracknell. When offered a position of a laboratory technician with a local experimental division of ICI, I accepted. Good money, promising career structure and being involved in what would prove to be a vital technology of the future – semiconductors. The position was subject to some very achievable exam results. My decision was reinforced by the mock exam assessment of my performance and the likelihood of gaining good results in the actual GCE exams.

The school format was to review and discuss in detail how to improve our performance after every mock exam. With the appropriate teacher we would also discuss what subjects should form the basis of an A level curriculum. Similar to today, there was a divide between the sciences, the arts and languages. After these reviews I was neither confident nor optimistic.

At that time, I was clueless as to my future ambitions. Richard knew what he wanted to do, but for me there seemed to be a complete mismatch between ambition and reality.

During an end of year woodwork exam, we were given 2 hours to make a dovetail joint. Most of us ended up creating some semblance of a joint. Richard spent the time manufacturing two pointed wooden sticks. On presentation, and after much bewilderment, the teacher looked Richard in the eye and said to him, 'whatever you do with your career, please make sure it has nothing to do with using your hands.' Richard's career for over 30 years was as a successful dentist!

My tongue

French was my weakest subject, but a chance encounter with a very attractive French exchange student at a youth club disco would enhance my chances of exam success. She was a couple of years older than me, and after a few dances, I invited her to have a drink at the Horse and Groom pub. After a few drinks I escorted her to where she was lodging, only to be told that entry was forbidden by her hosts. To my unexpected pleasure, during a snogging session outside the front door, she kept poking her tongue down my throat, which I thought was most odd. I had heard about French kissing, but this was for real. Her English was good , and it wasn't very long before I had the invitation to stuff my tongue down her throat. What I didn't expect was the massive amount of suction [Dyson would be envious] that she could generate.

This led to me generating a loud TWANG as the ligaments under my tongue snapped. Not a great deal of pain, but there was a small amount of bleeding. Resuming the passionate encounter, my main concern afterwards was that I could not control the movement of my tongue. Undeterred, with as deep and emotional voice that I could muster, a longing stare into her eyes (I also thought about becoming an actor), I delivered in my best French accent the killer line: '*Je t'aime.*' At this she placed her finger over my lips and said, 'Non, non.' She then proceeded in giving me a lesson in correct pronunciation. How to ruin a romantic moment with a lovely French girl. Unexpectedly, she did agree to see me again.

During her short stay we did continue our relationship, culminating with her attending with the rest of the French visitors the Ranelagh school swimming gala. It was held in the open air at the unheated Bracknell public swimming baths in May. The senior school – the fifth and sixth forms – were all competing in the various swimming events. My French belle and her friends created quite a stir with the senior boys of the sixth form by just being there. Before long the French girls became the centre of attention and conversation. There was a stunned silence when my girlfriend came over to where we lowly juniors were sitting and gave me a warm embrace and a long kiss (without tongues) in front of the whole senior school. Immediately my reputation within the school as a Romeo reached stratospheric proportions.

Back to the exams, and you would have thought that spending time with a French girlfriend would give me top marks in the oral part of the French GCE exam. No such luck. The format of the interview was to converse only in French. I was asked to enter a shop and buy a cravat (tie). So far, so good. Things started to deteriorate when I said in French that I was going to try the cravat on my tête. I was oblivious to my error even when interrupted with various growls and physical gestures by the examiner. Eventually he became increasingly agitated and asked me to get out and not come back. I had a fairly strong suspicion that a failure in the oral part of my French exam was on the cards.

The GCE exams were over a fairly short but intense period, with some days there being an exam in the morning and another in the afternoon. Did I have the mental stamina to concentrate for these lengthy periods – 3 hours per exam, sometimes twice a day? My solution was to drink strong coffee – extra caffeine had done me well in my 11+ exams, so I decided to use the same method again and dosed myself up just before each exam. It became apparent that I was on autopilot during the majority of the exams, especially the French. After each paper, when my classmates asked the usual question: 'How did you get on?', my reply was mostly: 'I haven't got a clue' – and that was being truthful. Having secured a job, without the need for great GCEs, there was also a certain degree of ambivalence on my part on how well I had performed.

My parent's ambition at that time was for me to leave school, leave further education and to settle into a real job with regular wages. There were comments like 'Why don't you become a butcher like John over the road, as people are always going to need meat?'. Social mobility was not a concept that most working-class folk on the estate considered, let alone discussed as a possibility.

The day of the GCE results arrived, and the Ranelagh policy was for each examinee to be given details of our exam results – by letter, by telephone or in person. In my case, the results were to be delivered face to face by the headmaster.

I roared up the long school drive and parked my newly acquired Lambretta Li 175cc directly in front of the large impressive front doors of school. Although this was breaking the rules, it didn't really matter because I was prepared for the very strong likelihood that this would be my last visit to the school.

On entering his study, the first thing the Beak asked of me was what were the subjects that I would be selecting for my sixth form 'A Level' studies. To say I was perplexed was an understatement. He then announced that I had passed all eight GCE subjects and rattled off my grades. Having recovered my senses, I suggested that he had got my name confused with another pupil and that there was no way that I could have passed French. On confirmation of a clean sweep, we agreed on Physics, Chemistry and Zoology. Driving home I did punch the air for joy and for the next few days had a huge grin from ear to ear.

While I was leaving his study, the Beak noticed that I was limping. This was due to my sports master trying to teach me to play tennis. He thought I had potential after nearly beating one of the school team players. On lunging for a volley, I had damaged my left knee, resulting in pain and swelling. Up to then years of high impact sport and not so much as a sprain. I explained that my family doctor said that the knee would most likely require surgery. Now that I was staying on at school and being a key player in most of the school teams, especially rugby, the Beak was horrified that I would not be fit for the new rugby season, which was only a couple of months away. He said: 'Leave it to me', and sure enough, within a few days (I don't know how he managed it) an appointment for an operation at Heatherwood Hospital, Ascot was sent to me.

My perceived future had taken its first unexpected and decisive change in direction. I was now set for an academic/professional career, but in what? I had plenty of time to consider my options but discussions with my parents provided little guidance. Their lack of understanding didn't help the discussions. As I was the first in the history of the family to enter further education, there was little to guide us. Before long it seemed that I was getting advice from every passing adult, including most of the neighbours. A consensus developed, centred around the advantages of being part of a profession with a specialisation. With that in mind and none the wiser, I decided to focus on enjoying the present situation and let the universe decide for me.

The decision to stay on at school meant that instead of starting work immediately as a laboratory technician working for ICI, which my parents would have preferred, I could now look forward to a long summer holiday with not a care in the world. Although I intended to continue the gardening job, I applied for the position of assistant caretaker at my school. I was given the job and was soon turning up at school as an employee. This entailed spending three days a week cleaning and polishing the floors of the classrooms, toilets and corridors for the duration of the school summer holiday.

For most of the time I was on my own, having the luxury of being able to listen to uninterrupted music on my portable radio. Other advantages were better money than landscape gardening, only working weekdays and convenient hours, allowing more time for fishing. After the summer holidays the job morphed into being an after-school cleaner for 2 hours immediately after classes had finished. When cleaning the toilets, I would often catch kids in the act of smoking or other nefarious activities. As a sixth former and a prefect, I would read the riot act, but didn't think it necessary to either discipline or report them.

At the beginning of 1967 could anyone, including me, have predicted that by the summer, I would have eight GCEs under my belt and a likely future that was not going to be entirely dependent on sheer hard work and industry? Coming from a working-class environment and with most of my estate friends leaving their respective schools for work or apprenticeships, I struggled to envisage the near future that would involve further full-time education. Despite these diverging circumstances we as a group of friends decided to continue our friendships much the same as before.

Although I had never been one to focus on any particular issues in the media, 1967 brought an increasing atmosphere of global angst. Politics were getting darker and conflicts all around the world were becoming more extreme and polarised. Again Vietnam, the Cold War, social inequalities and racism were being reported on a daily basis. I believe my generation's reaction to these adversities was demonstrated by being proactively involved in Peace rallies and Flower Power.,. All genres of pop, rock, blues and folk music were reflecting and challenging to the existing status quo of society. I considered myself to be of an age where acceptance of handed down beliefs should be challenged.

While working on a landscape gardening job, I happened to notice that the adjacent building appeared to house lots of young mums, many of whom were pushing prams with their babies. I asked the guy working with me what was going on. He told me that it was a home/refuge for single unmarried mothers. Although appearing to me to be a man of the world, well balanced and intelligent, he implied that these women were from unfortunate circumstances and immoral. He also implied that these women were slightly subnormal and had to be kept away from society together with their babies. At the time, I did not have any notion of the terrible plight young unmarried girls faced over being socially stigmatised. It wasn't until the 1970s that I realised the huge pain and suffering inflicted on future generations by this barbaric treatment of the young and unmarried, especially when many were forced into having their babies adopted.

While staying in the orthopaedic ward in Heatherwood Hospital, I noticed that many of my fellow patients were recovering from motorcycle accidents, some having lost limbs or sustained other life-changing injuries. This gave me a valuable lesson in the dangers and consequences of driving a motorised two-wheeler. The instabilities of my motor scooter made it dangerous enough, without adding to the risk with any foolhardy behaviour. For me heavy drinking was confined to trips taken on foot, using public transport or as a passenger in a car.

This was also the year when Barclays Bank introduced cash machines. For me and many of my peers, cash was the only form of currency. Having received cash for working, it was the only fiscal method available. Credit cards and bank accounts were for the future. I did open my first bank account in 1969 ready for university. It was with Barclays bank. I then became one of the early users of a credit card – Barclaycard.

The news was starting to filter through with the less glorious aspect of the Vietnam war, including the Vinh Xuen massacre. It was also revealed that the US army was using banned germ and chemical warfare, as well as indiscriminate carpet bombing. No wonder many of the public in the USA were anti-war. To make the geopolitical tensions worse, China exploded its first hydrogen bomb. On visiting my family dentist, in the autumn of '67, I read an article in *Time* magazine describing how the communists in China and North Vietnam would sweep through the Pacific to invade Australia, very much like the Japanese in the Second World War.

In the USA, both massive anti-Vietnam and race riots were spreading throughout the country, despite 1967 being known as the 'Summer of Love'.

In 1976, I was reminded of the events of 1967 and the Arab–Israeli war, when I was invited to fly to the Scilly Isles in a small private aircraft. On entering the plane, I noticed lines of patched welding along the fuselage. I asked my Round Table pilot friend what and why they were there. The plane had been used by Moshe Dayan, Minister of Defence and architect of the Arab defeat. The patches were the repairs to the bullet holes received during the war. Moshe Dayan also had a patch, but over his lost left eye. He lost it in 1941, fighting in Syria. During our flight we were not shot at, and our passage in the air was uneventful. Landing at St Mary's airport was however a jaw-clenching experience. On landing, our inexperienced pilot hoped that the brakes would work as the runway was short and an over-run would mean tipping the plane into the sea.

One of the all-time classics from the Bee Gees, 'Massachusetts' was released in 1967. In November, Bee Gees member, Robin Gibb survived the Hither Green rail crash which killed 49 people.

On 1 July came the launch of colour TV, with Wimbledon being shown on BBC 2. As a family we didn't regard watching tennis in colour sufficient motivation for buying a new expensive television.

Of greater concern to me was the banning of offshore radio stations, especially Radio Caroline and London. These were my main sources of good pop music. Fortunately, by the end of September the launch of BBC's Radio 1 proved for me to be a great alternative. When Tony Blackburn opened the very first show with The Move's 'Flowers in the Rain', I thought this was a really good choice as the song was one of a batch of Flower Power/ Psychedelic releases that reflected the Hippie Culture. An added bonus was that the signal being transmitted by the BBC was so much more powerful, meaning the reception to my transistor radio was vastly improved.

* * *

After the GCE exam results, there was a rash of school parties. Much of the music being played would reflect the 'Summer of Love' and the drug inspired psychedelic classics:

'Purple Haze' 'A Day in the Life' (Banned by BBC) Jimi Hendrix

'A Whiter Shade of Pale' – Procol Harum

'See Emily Play' – Pink Floyd

'Itchycoo Park' – Small Faces

'Paper Sun' / 'Hole in My Shoe' – Traffic

'A Day in the Life' (Banned by BBC) / 'All You Need Is Love'

The soundtrack of the Summer of Love – *Sgt. Pepper's Lonely Hearts Club Band*

'Let's Go To San Francisco' – Flowerpot Men. Peace and Love.

'San Francisco' – Scott McKenzie. Peace and Love.

'Light My Fire' – the Doors

'Ruby Tuesday' / 'Let's Spend the Night Together'

Much of this music was setting the scene for smooching, slow dancing, alcohol and smoking substances that had a distinctive smell. I never minded or objected others indulging in the weed, but I was never tempted. The various effects of alcohol were enough for me.

When the exams were over virtually the entire school fifth form was in party mode. Girls who I considered plain now, seen in trendy attire, became attractive. I attended these parties with a sense of sensual excitement fuelled by the evocative music. My own party outfit was a very tight-fitting purple crepe shirt with even tighter fitting white flared hipsters. The only let down was my school haircut.

It is easy to forget that besides the 'flower power' and drug inspired music, 1967 was also a phenomenal year for pop music of all genres. The list is seemingly endless, but here's a few of my favourites at the time.

Box Tops – 'The Letter'

The Mamas & The Papas – 'Dedicated to the One I Love'

The Turtles – 'Happy Together' and 'She'd Rather Be With Me'

Eddie Floyd – 'Knock on Wood'

Lulu – 'To Sir With Love'. From the film of the same title.

The Easybeats – 'Friday on My Mind'

Arthur Conley – 'Sweet Soul Music'

Brenton Wood – 'Gimme Little Sign'

Tremeloes – 'Silence is Golden'

Aretha Franklin – 'Respect'

Cat Stevens – 'Mathew and Son'

The Beatles – 'The Fool On The Hill'. So relevant today.

Long John Baldry – 'Let the Heartaches Begin'

The parties together with the fantastic music would continue throughout the summer, only to be curtailed by the return to school and the commencing of the A level syllabus.

The blue rowing boat

With the exams the exams finishing, we were free to enjoy the new fishing season. Frank and I, given the right conditions on the Thames, would bunk off from our respective schools for an angling session at our favourite venues of Wargrave and Shiplake. When there were sunny conditions, the fishing would slow in the backwater. Knowing that for most of the afternoon the fishing wouldn't improve, we were left wondering where to try next. Although upstream the river Loddon was an option, just downstream of the boatyard was an enticing stretch of river that was only accessible by boat. We asked Len Bushnell if any of his collection of dinghies, skiffs and punts, which were stored under the shelter of the railway bridge, could be repurposed by us for fishing. He pointed out a small wooden rowing boat that needed some attention to make it shipshape and watertight. If we were prepared to do the work, we were welcome to use it. It was a fun project, and in no time the dinghy was ready to be used. Soon Frank and I were sitting side by side, fishing in our chosen spot on the mainstream. For anchorage we had filled two paint cans with concrete, which proved more than adequate for the task.

It was a small dinghy, but with a certain amount of coordination, we managed to keep our lines from getting entangled with each other – well, most of the time. On one occasion our floats were particularly close, and both disappeared under the surface simultaneously. To our surprise we were both fighting a good fish. Once the surface of the water was broken by a very large perch, the realisation dawned that we had both hooked the same fish. As usual, a discussion followed over who hooked the fish first and who could claim it as theirs. We agreed to disagree and continued to catch fish separately.

Our small dinghy gave us a completely new perspective over the possible venues we could access and explore. After much discussion, the fast and deep water of the Loddon was to be our next target venue, not only for the fishing but also to explore the natural beauty of the river.

Passing fascinating views of the amazing bank side houses with beautiful gardens, we decided to come ashore. Because of the high steep banks, finding a spot to moor up was a challenge. Eventually a perfect spot was found where we could climb onto the bank as well as securing the boat. As I was tethering the rope to a branch of an overhanging tree, Frank decided to jump back into the boat to fetch some of our fishing gear. The sound of splitting wood was ominous, as a large wooden stake appeared in the centre of the boat. Frank frantically handed me our fishing tackle as the boat filled with water and quickly sank. All was saved except for one of the oars. I was still holding the rope to prevent the boat from being washed downstream, when Frank without a word of explanation, set off like a wild deranged thing, climbed the bank and thundered along in pursuit of the oar. Thump, thump, thump followed by an almighty splash!

Frank had plunged into 6 feet of deep, fast-flowing water. I shouted several times with no response. Eventually managing to secure the boat, I slowly walked along the bank to find out if Frank was either alive or to be found floating face down several miles downstream in Henley weir pool. To my relief, he was clinging to tufts of grass, completely immersed in river water and without the means of climbing onto the bank. He was staring up at me in a state of shock and disbelief but holding the missing oar. After hauling him to safety, all I could think of was 'phew!' Although the dinghy was over a hundred years old, and beautifully built, Len Bushnell was seemingly unperturbed that we had wrecked it. We felt that it would be only politic to curtail our fishing boat trips for the foreseeable future.

Heatherwood hospital

Following my express referral, the time had arrived to have my knee operation. This was the first time that I was to be put under the knife since having my tonsils extracted aged 5. I remember waking up after the operation with a massive pressure bandage on my left leg. The plan was to operate on the injured knee, and to make sure, there was a very clear red arrow painted on my upper left thigh. Although relieved that the correct leg had been operated on, there was an impressive level of pain from the operation site. Next to the bed, in a jar, was a chunk of bone that had been floating around my knee joint. The nurse that first attended my bedside informed me that it was the cause of my previous pain and swelling and suggested that I could keep it as a trophy.

Although still a bit woozy after the anaesthetic, I vaguely recognised the pretty nurse who was attending me. I asked her if we had ever met before. She answered in the affirmative, saying we had met at the Thing a Me Jig club in Reading and that I had subsequently stood her up. Oops.

This didn't seem to affect her nursing care of me, but she wouldn't give me a second chance to date her.

I had been placed in an orthopaedic ward, and being an open ward, I quickly got to know my neighbours. To my left was a young guy who was recovering from a motorbike accident. He was very handsome, and he knew it. To my right was a thickset military type, a sergeant serving in the Coldstream Guards (the ones who dress up with big black hairy hats and parade outside Buckingham Palace, etc). He was recovering from a leg operation and seemed to be having special care from an attractive Sister in charge of the ward. In front of the rest of us patients, he would be wheeled to the shower room for special attention. They would then both disappear for up to half an hour. My suspicions were aroused when they both reappeared with broad smiles and Sister's uniform needed rearranging.

After a few days on the ward, the leg pain diminished and with my trusty radio I was able to listen to the great songs that were in the charts. 'Lucy in the Sky with Diamonds' together with other songs from *Sgt. Pepper's Lonely Hearts Club Band*, 'A Whiter Shade of Pale' (Procol Harum), 'Purple Haze' (Jimi Hendrix), and many more of my favourites. We very quickly organised a fairly serious card school. One of our players had one arm; the other had been chopped off in an alleged hospital mix-up. He was philosophical about it. Servings of hospital sandwiches washed down with our daily bottle of Guinness made our time pass relatively comfortably.

After ten largely pleasant days, it felt a bit strange that I was leaving the hospital to join the world outside. After being 'institutionalised', I had the feeling both that it was time to resume my life, and that there was time lost to make up for. However, with a long holiday to look forward to, and the next stage of my life more or less sorted, as a sixth-former, a great sense of optimism and gratitude pervaded my thoughts. With knee fixed, all activities – sport, riding my scooter, dancing and walking to my favourite fishing spots – could resume.

As soon as my knee allowed, I decided to put my life into fourth gear – very few cars had five gears in the '60s. Besides the cleaning job, I worked on a few building sites and, of course, landscape gardening. Engel increased my pay and asked me to consider becoming a partner, if I decided not to go to university. I did consider his proposal, especially as I did love manual labour and working outside close to nature. There were negatives to consider, such as the winter months and bad weather, which at any time of year could prevent me earning money. Other considerations were that there would be little career structure and the success of the business couldn't be assumed. As it turned out, I would have been very wealthy at a relatively young age: Engel's landscape gardening business grew and became successful enough to allow him to retire early. He would repeat his generous offer right up to the time I left for Bristol University and his honest work ethic stayed with me always.

Sometimes an illness and/or a spell of confinement can be cathartic. At the time my thoughts were more about how much I was missing my social life. After all, it was my school holidays. The spell in hospital gave time to examine my lifestyle more objectively. Girlfriend[s] were occupying too much of my time and I realised that having steady relationships was not for me. Within a week of returning home, I was single again.

On one occasion after coming home from hospital, I was feeling sorry for myself so I decided to accept an invitation to Jim's party. I knew that there would not be any unattached girls there, so when I arrived, I decided to drink whatever was put in front of me, aided and assisted by Jim's father. We discussed the meaning of life and together sampled rare whiskies and spirit-based cocktails. My last memory was of being sat in an armchair with a bottle of Cinzano in one hand and a sick bag in the other. I have never been able to drink the stuff since.

On awakening early next morning, I was unable to move; the feeling of being paralysed from the neck down scared me. For a short time, I couldn't move my head or speak. It seemed that death was close at hand. Richard and I, studying chemistry and zoology, had often discussed the effects of excessive alcohol on the body and the brain. Beyond the anaesthetic effects of too much alcohol, the next phase was an ascending paralysis of the nervous system, becoming unable to breathe. It was a close-run thing that night. Lesson learned.

Recovering from my drunken night, I needed to rebalance my thoughts about a carefree lifestyle. My immediate resolution was to take schoolwork and sport more seriously, and dare I say it, a greater commitment to fishing with my mates.

Back to school and there were now only three main subjects, though I was now met with an immediate increase in the length and difficulty of homework. I could cope with Chemistry and Zoology, but the maths involvement with Physics was beyond me. Some of my brainy classmates could solve these complex equations in a few minutes. I would consider myself lucky if after hours of effort any of the questions were answered correctly. I have always wondered what happened to those bright sparks end up and what work they do.

Michaelmas term, the start of the new academic year, brought with it unexpected school sports achievements in rugby and basketball. It was the year that sporting achievements were to reach a level rarely obtained by a small school. Although the total pool of boys in both upper and lower sixth forms were less than seventy, the upper sixth had a disproportionate number of very good and gifted athletes. Our rugby 1st team was winning most matches comfortably, but it was the basketball team that was having stratospheric results. Of a pool of ten, myself and 'Mac' McLean stood at 5 ft 10 ins, 'the shorties'; the next 'shortest' were 6 ft 2 ins and 6 ft 4 ins respectively, the rest of them being even taller, topping out at 6 ft 7 ins. To improve our technique and skill levels, the sports master, Norm, brought in an American basketball coach for a few training sessions. We were locally unbeatable and reached the national schools semi-finals of the U18's basketball, narrowly being beaten by the eventual winners. Two of our stars started playing semi-professional after leaving school.

In contrast the following year it was my turn to take over the captaincy of both school teams. The results under my leadership were a disaster. Being a little disillusioned, I turned my attention to sporting activities outside of school, such as playing rugby for Bracknell seniors and captaining Bracknell Colts.

Most of our estate gang now had a variety of motorised transport. Frank had been given a brand new Lambretta Li 150; Jim, a 50cc Mope; Giles, a Vespa 125 scooter; while neighbour John's friend Stephen, who was older, had a red Austin 1275cc Mini Cooper S. We now could regularly travel to our favourite places. Several of these were in Reading which became our go-to place. The Thing A Me Jig club was our favourite nightclub playing great music. Reading's Majestic Ballroom would hold regular dances with famous music acts such as the legendary Geno Washington & the Ram Jam Band. When invited to ride in the Cooper S with its phenomenal acceleration and handling, I would feel slick and very trendy, rolling up to the nightclub with my image enhanced by wearing my purple fur coat and matching tight fitting trousers and crepe shirt.

On reflection the Thing A Me Jig club was a real change from the existing format of nightclubs because it was exclusively a discotheque as opposed to having live music. Besides being a good venue for meeting girls, it was a great place to dance and listen to Black and Motown classics such as 'Road Runner', 'Knock on Wood, 'I Can't Help Myself (Sugar Pie, Honey Bunch)', 'Sweet Soul Music', 'Respect' plus slow dancing to classic smoochers such as 'My Girl', 'A Whiter Shade of Pale' and 'When a Man Loves a Woman'. For me, the music, atmosphere and vibe of disco type nightclubs were becoming etched into my teenage psyche and would continue well after university.

Having the freedom of transport, we travelled on a whim to Bognor Regis and spent the evening at a nightclub. As it was a fine night we decided to sleep on the beach and sunbathe in the morning. Why Bognor? Perhaps it was the name. We also planned visits to The Crown at Pishill and the Gate at Bryants Bottom. Sometimes after the pubs closed and not wanting the evening to end, we would drive to the newly opened Little Chef on the A30 in Bagshot. Open until late this was the place to go. We would often be met by hordes of bikers and revellers about to attend the nearby Pantiles nightclub.

The Pantiles building was used in the film *Reach for the Sky* and was the tea shop where it is said Sir Douglas Bader met his future wife, Thema. Fortunately, my neighbour and older friend John was a member of the prestigious Pantiles nightclub, so occasionally I entered its hallowed doors as his guest. It was run like a posh West End nightclub, but in Surrey. Attendees and performers were the likes of Alan Price, Long John Baldry, Georgie Fame and groups like Fleetwood Mac, Chicken Shack, Geno Washington & the Ram Jam band, plus a plethora of world-famous celebrities. Partly due to my age and background I felt intimidated by the sophisticated atmosphere of the club.

By the closing months of 1967, my 'Road Runner' sabbatical, was still in place. My decision to spend more time with my mates for both sport, fishing and social activities was paying dividends in unusual ways. Time spent with Richard meant time to explore our future careers. Richard would often discuss possible jobs and professions that might appeal to me. For some reason, Richard was already focused and had settled upon being a dentist. When I asked him about his choice, he couldn't give me any tangible answers but never waived from his future career path. I was ambiguous and if I had been asked in a careers interview, my response would have been a shrug of the shoulders. At that moment in time my only criteria were that I enjoyed working with people and something involving biological processes. Then fate pointed the way for me, in a genuine piece of synchronicity.

My introduction to dentistry

In all the bruising games of rugby, I had yet to sustain a significant injury. However, a friendly gentle tap on my lower jaw by one of my rugby teammates caused me to clamp my teeth together, resulting in my upper right incisors snapping just above the gum line. Not a lot of pain, but as this accident happened at school, the Beak immediately sent me to a private dentist for emergency treatment. After waiting for more than two hours, I was invited into a dimly lit, posh surgery with soft music playing in the background. Without a greeting or word of explanation, my two fractured front teeth were cut down to be level with the gum. This was painful enough because the drill cut through my live nerves. Then the real pain followed when a barbed needle was inserted into the bleeding nerve chamber to literally pull out the remaining live tissue. I can remember very vividly the pain. Having very little experience of dental treatment, I assumed naïvely that this was normal private dentistry – all done without any form of anaesthetic!

I was then turfed out of the surgery and told to continue treatment with my family dentist. Faced with a whooping gap at the front of my mouth and two dead tooth roots that quickly started smelling putrid, I made an appointment to see my family's dentist who was a traditional, caring NHS dental practitioner. He also employed a pleasant dental nurse who made my visits more comfortable by smiling and holding my hand when I was sat in the chair. Although this was not the most auspicious introduction to what would be a 40-year plus career with teeth and gums, this horrific experience did steer a pathway towards it.

Although I still had freedom of choice, there was now a shift in my conscious decision making, and a future in dentistry became a distinct possibility.

> 'Now there's more to do than watch my sailboat glide
> And every day can be my magic carpet ride.'
> 'Goin' Back'

The year ended with the death of one my favourite soul singers, the great Otis Redding. He had just written and recorded 'Sittin' On The Dock of the Bay', which went on to be a mega hit in 1968 and beyond. To me he was the voice of soul in the '60s. Many of the songs he recorded such as 'Mr Pitiful', 'I've Been Loving You Too Long', 'Respect', 'These Arms of Mine', 'My Girl', and 'Try a Little Tenderness' epitomise the magic of these years, my relationships with girls and the accompanying emotions of the time. Whenever I listen to the first few bars of 'Dock of the Bay', even today, the memories and accompanying emotions come flooding back.

1968

The year began with my immediate priority to have some visible front teeth. To this effect, I attended the family dental practice regularly to change the disinfectant dressing on the paper points that had been placed inside the nerve chambers of the infected dead front teeth. For what appeared to be an eternity, the taste and smell from these teeth was stubbornly resistant to the dentist's treatment. Although this procedure was completely painless, it wasn't as efficient as the treatments of today. At these appointments, my dentist would ceremoniously pull out the paper points with tweezers and sniff them. Very much like a master of wine would smell the cork of a newly opened bottle of fine wine – instead, he was a master of detecting the distinct aroma of infection. Some dentists can even tell the type of bacteria by their smell.

Eventually the dentist was happy that there wasn't any active infection, primarily by the absence of pus and the associated smell. Not being confident in completing the root canal therapy (RCT), he was prepared to fit some temporary crowns. When the temps were fitted, they were made from hollow plastic stock teeth. These crowns were fixed onto my tooth stumps with posts and a weak dental cement. To facilitate easy removal the posts were made of sawn-off paper clips. From a cosmetic standpoint the colour of the crowns was a ridiculous shade of pale yellow and a complete shape mismatch to my natural teeth. They did, however, fill the gap for what turned out to be the next couple of years. Additionally, stability was not their greatest attribute and they would often fall out without warning. This did not help my confidence, especially when being in the company of potential girlfriends.

Most of the dances and nightclubs that I attended were using an ultraviolet light to magnify the whiteness of clothing and human tissues such as teeth. Yes, you have guessed it, my front teeth looked like a magnified patchwork of colours from black, brown, yellow and brilliant white.

During my lunch break in a trendy café in Reading where I was working at the time, I started a conversation with a wonderful looking girl who seemed genuinely interested in me. As I was about to ask her for a date, there was the sound of an ominous metallic clunk on my food tray. To my shame and horror, I was staring down at my false front tooth with a sawn-off paper clip sticking out of it. By any standards, this was not a pretty sight. Before she noticed I clamped my hand to cover the errant tooth, and used my other hand to cover my mouth and started speaking like a ventriloquist. As I felt more like the dummy, my only option was to discreetly pick up the tooth, mumble my excuses and leave.

I had to wait until 1970, when I was a dental student at Bristol Dental School before the two front teeth were permanently root-filled, and permanent posts and porcelain crowns fitted. At last, these crowns matched the colour and shape of the rest of the teeth in my mouth.

Current affairs

I was becoming more interested in current affairs and the year started with a ridiculous campaign called 'I'm Backing Britain'. Coming from a working-class background, I found being asked to work extra hours for no extra pay, to help the UK's balance of payments, both derisory and laughable. The media really got behind the idea with the likes of Bruce Forsyth releasing the song 'I'm Backing Britain'. A certain Jimmy Saville worked for nine days at Leeds Royal Infirmary as a porter without claiming a fee. He then boasted that this was the equivalent of £30,000 in his 'real job'.

The first signs of decimalisation started to creep in this year by introducing a 5p coin (shilling) and a 10p coin (florin). Although I was aware of many of these potentially significant political, financial and social changes at the time, my life was too hectic to be overly concerned. There were times when these subjects would become a topic of conversation. Mainly when we had nothing better to talk about over a pint in the pub.

There were some news events that did pique my interest:

Manchester United was the first English team to win the European Cup: Benfica 1 – Manchester United 4.

The London's East End's Kray brothers Ronnie, Reggie and Charlie, were arrested and charged with murder, fraud, blackmail and assault, just to name a few of their crimes.

The Race Relations Act became law. This was quite an achievement especially after the infamous 'Rivers of Blood' speech by Enoch Powell.

Influenza Pandemic 1968–1971

By the middle of the year, I was hearing about Hong Kong Flu (H3N2) via snippets on the TV, radio and newspapers. The West were blaming the Chinese and calling it 'Mao Flu'. My family, friends, school and all social contacts appeared to be oblivious of the fact that this was an ancestor of the devastating Spanish Flu (H1N1) of 1918/19.

At the time, due to its deadly symptoms, the World Health Organization (WHO) rapidly announced this flu outbreak as a global pandemic. The only other declared influenza pandemic of the 20th century started in mid-1957 and was over by mid-1958 and was labelled Asian Flu (H2N2). Although a very conservatively estimated 20,000 in the UK, 80,000 in the USA, and over 1 million Worldwide died from Asian Flu of 1957, there were few hysterical media headlines or calls for masks and social distancing. The same was true for the more deadly 1968 version.

The 1968 Hong Kong Flu has now been largely forgotten; even though it raged until 1971 and killed many more than the estimated 30,000 UK, 100,000 USA and 4 million Worldwide. (I am sure that my illness in 1970 at the start of my university attendance was this influenza – I was advised to take to my bed and sleep it off.) Unlike today, over 50% of fatalities were under 65 years old. In December 1968, the *New York Times* called the pandemic as 'one of the worst in the nation's history'. Interestingly, a few months after the pandemic was declared, the Woodstock festival became one of the largest music festivals in history. Over half a million 'love and peace hippies' were gathered at a dairy farm in Bethel, New York. Many regard the gathering as the defining event for the 'Counterculture generation. A few months later the Motarorium March in Washington DC, where over half a million people protesting in the largest anti-war demonstration in the history of the USA, again all took place when the global pandemic was raging without any mandates blocking public gatherings.

Globally, 1968 turned out to be one of the most turbulent years of the decade. The mood of love and peace of '67, was rapidly being replaced by public anger, indignation and in some cases, disbelief, especially among the young and liberal intellectuals. Mass demonstrations, riots and protests were happening all over the World, sometimes fuelled by an ever-growing presence of the media. The Prague Spring, a revolt against Soviet domination was crushed by a massive Communist force; and massacres in Vietnam were examples of on-the-spot video news coverage being shown to a massive audience via television.

One of my favourite subjects at school was history. My teacher was a great advocate of cause and effect-based learning. Instead of just reeling off dates, facts and figures, he would discuss the background social, political and monetary factors driving events, no matter how seemingly unrelated these causative influences were.

Taking a historical and objective analysis of the information being presented, I would assess and try to place virtually everything that was espoused by government and all forms of associated media with a new perspective. I would challenge or doubt any announcement or news feature where there were viewpoints that didn't seem to make sense.

On reflection my history teacher was a great help to my education. He did go 'off piste' from the prescribed educational doctrine. As the song goes, 'One less brick in the wall.'

Looking back, it wasn't just me, but a quantum shift in my generation's acceptance of the status quo that were challenging governments throughout the world.

The murder of Martin Luther King, shot down by James Earl Ray on 4 April, as with John F Kennedy, shocked the world. There were riots all over the world from all sectors of the public and protests from musicians like Nina Simone and James Brown. The My Lai Massacre were hundreds of women, children, and old men were slaughtered, was a major turning point in the public's support for the war in Vietnam; followed again by mass riots and demonstrations. Robert Kennedy, a supporter of Israel, was assassinated , apparently by a Palestinian – but that motive was seen by the sceptical as too obvious; was the man arrested just the fall guy? The term 'conspiracy theory' was commonly used after the John Kennedy assassination.

The entertainment industry reflected the mood of the times and changing society, with films, musicals, plays and of course songs.

The Graduate, one of my favourites, is widely regarded as being one of the culturally and historically significant films of the decade. It resonated with me as it satirises the alienation of the youth of the day. The poignancy of the words of 'The Sound of Silence' and 'Mrs Robinson' led to reviewing my perception of the changing world of 1968 and made me try to understand the deeper consequences of the evolving social change. Both film and songs made a greater psychological impact.

There were an amazing number of great films released during this period and looking back to my favourites, I can see where my head was at: *Night of the Living Dead*, *Rosemary's Baby*, *The Devil Rides Out*, *Up the Junction*, *2001: A Space Odyssey* and *Yellow Submarine* to name a few.

Because there were no video players, let alone Netflix, many popular films like the Spaghetti Western series would be re-released at the local cinemas.

With the relaxation of censorship came full-frontal nudity. The musical *Hair* broke new ground as a 'rock musical' with sex, drugs, anti-Vietnam War dialogue, long hair – and the audience able to speculate on the religion of the male actors.

My new love – the West Country

My favourite A level subject was Zoology, especially the practical classes involving observation and involvement with living creatures. Part of the first year's curriculum was to attend a residential zoological field course. I chose a newly created ecology and environmental course at Nettlecombe Court. It was situated in a Tudor country mansion on the edge of Exmoor National Park near Williton, Somerset, a part of the country about which I knew little.

A coach had been organised to transport the students from my region to the centre. To save money and for a bit of adventure, I decided to leave a day earlier, hitch-hike to Bristol, spend the night there, and travel onward to Williton. The main route to Bristol from Bracknell was via the A4 road; the M4, which now connects London to Bristol, was only just being built.

Having been transported by a kindly lorry driver for about half my journey, I found myself in the remote wilds of Wiltshire with little passing traffic. One of my all-time favourite cars, a Triumph TR5, approached me, and I couldn't believe my luck when it stopped and a smart, good-looking, young man offered to take me the rest of the way to the centre of Bristol. Guy and I became immediate friends. He was a young and successful sales manager for all sorts of white goods and recommended Bristol as a great city to attend university. He would later introduce me to the Mandrake Club, which was not only the best nightclub in the city when I was a student, but also provided me with a regular job as bartender and DJ. After dropping me off in the centre of Bristol, Guy suggested that I might find a B&B along the adjacent dockside area.

I was immediately captivated by my brief exploration of the historic parts of the city centre and the dockside area. As if by magic, I came across a doorway advertising low-cost accommodation. A very pleasant lady with a thick Bristolian accent showed me to a room with an enormous bed. 'You'll be sleeping in the same bed as that Humphry Davy fella,' she said and wished me well. My sleep was enchanted, almost as if the room was sending me a message.

I was studying Chemistry and Physics, so Sir Humphry Davy was a legend. The man who invented electrochemistry and the Davy Lamp (a safety lamp for use in mines), coined the term 'laughing gas' and isolated many chemical elements for the first time, was also a poet, with friends such as William Wordsworth, Samuel Taylor Coleridge and Robert Southey. When I woke up in Humphry Davy's bed, I knew that Bristol was to be my number one choice of universities and, second, that any career that I followed would be based on evidence-based science. With that settled and after a hearty breakfast, I continued my travels into the wilds of Somerset.

I managed to reach the prearranged meeting place in the pretty village of Monksilver. Having arrived with plenty of time to spare, and now standing outside the village pub, I thought it would be ridiculous not to sample the local speciality, scrumpy cider. On entering the bar area, I asked for a pint of the draught cider which was on tap. Two of the regular old boys who were propped up at the bar shook their heads and recommended that I should try a half to start. I acknowledged their concern but continued with my initial order. The pint slipped down very well, with very little immediate side effects. On ordering the second pint, the locals became very concerned with my well-being and started shaking their heads. One of them looked at me and gave the sign of the Cross. On stepping outside to wait for the coach, I understood the reason for their warnings. At the first intake of fresh air, my legs gave way so that I could barely manage to crawl to a bench. How I managed to arrive at the centre without appearing completely inebriated and incapacitated is anyone's guess.

Despite my hungover state, I realised during the first evening meal that there were many attractive female attendees outnumbering the boys by a huge multiple: eight boys to forty-six girls. As a mixed residential course, the next few days would prove to be interesting, especially as the dormitory supervision was minimal.

Although the indoor class work consisted of relatively boring lectures, note taking and laboratory observations, the fantastic May weather and the outside field coursework created my perfect holiday – the educational part as a bonus. Trips into the wild and rugged Exmoor and collecting bugs in the local stream and woodland quickly enhanced my affection for that part of North Somerset. My euphoria was considerably enhanced by spending most of the evenings with a lovely girl from Portsmouth. Drunken visits to the pub and a constant supply of home-brewed scrumpy cider, supplied by the Centre's cook, created a constant party atmosphere. My highlight was catching beautiful, edible-sized brown trout in the local stream, for many of my newfound friends to eat in the Centre's kitchen, with new potatoes and washed down with cook's potent delicious cider. The happiest of days.

On my return to Bracknell, I reflected on the significance of the Somerset trip. It was the first time that I had spent time in a completely different educational environment. The realisation that it was possible for me to mix with a group of people of a similar age and academically similar interests had made the whole experience enjoyable and exciting. My confidence was at an all-time high, and all appeared to bode well for my decision to become a university undergraduate.

A new-found love of Bristol and all things West Country had cemented my determination of where I wanted to study. Now it was up to me to decide on a career which would involve utilising biological knowledge to help and treat people. As my friend and fishing buddy Richard had consistently voiced his determination to be a dentist, and with my front teeth requiring permanent root fillings and crowns, it seemed that the universe was pointing me in one direction. With that in mind, I thought of giving odontology a try. Little did I realise that over fifty years later dentistry would still be part of my life.

At the end of the summer term, the school organised a panoramic photograph of the entire school. We all had to be dressed immaculately in our school uniforms, with our hair combed and presentable. When the impressively large full colour photo of 400+ pupils and thirty+ teachers was pinned to the notice board, there was a veritable scrum to get a viewing, with howls of laughter. As a prefect, I asked a youngster what the fuss was about. He told me I should look at pupils at both ends of the photograph. After staring for a few minutes, I noticed that one of the school leavers, had stood at the left-hand side of the line-up, an image of dress perfection, only to reappear again at the other end – this time without a tie, jacket half off, hair sticking out at all angles and rolling his eyes so that only the whites were showing. I, like many others, thought this was hilarious. The Beak took a different view.

Although the pupil was leaving, his choices were either immediate expulsion or a severe caning.

Having sorted out my career pathway, I was able to focus and return to much more immediate and pressing issues: fishing, social activities and finding the funds to support them. 1968 was to be without any major exams to interrupt my calendar. The phenomenal music of that year had helped to create a truly momentous sense of appreciation for that period of my life. Looking back, I often ask myself, 'How did I fit it all in?'

* * *

The song list seems endless, but for me all have a special place in my memories. This was a time of nightclubs and discos.

The Beatles – 'Hey Jude', 'Magical Mystery Tour' (EP), *The White Album* and *Yellow Submarine* film

Simon and Garfunkel – 'Mrs Robinson', 'Scarborough Fair', *Bookends* album

Otis Redding – '(Sitting On) The Dock of the Bay', and *Dock of the Bay* the album. Both posthumous number one's records.

Glen Campbell – 'Wichita Lineman'

Vanilla Fudge – 'You Keep Me Hangin' On'. Slow heavy rock version of the Supremes hit.

The Moody Blues – 'Nights in White Satin'. Absolutely a classic.

Aretha Franklin – 'I Say a Little Prayer'. One of my all-time favourites.

Merrilee Rush – 'Angel of the Morning'

Bobby Goldsboro – 'Honey'

Cream – 'Sunshine of Your Love / White Room

Herb Albert – 'This Guy's in Love with *You'.* All-time great.

Hugo Montenegro – 'The Good, the Bad and the Ugly'

Tommy James and the Shondells – 'Mony Mony'

Sly & the Family Stone – 'Dance to the Music'

John Fred & his Playboy Band – "Judy in Disguise [With Glasses]'

Steppenwolf – 'Born to be Wild'

The Crazy World of Arthur Brown – 'Fire'

Rolling Stones – 'Jumpin' Jack Flash' and *Beggars Banquet* [album]

The Turtles – 'Elenore'

Richard Harris – 'MacArthur Park'

The Troggs – 'Love is All Around'

Jose Feliciano – 'Light My Fire'

Joe Cocker – 'With a Little Help from My Friends'

Jimi Hendrix – 'All Along the Watchtower'

The Small Faces – 'Lazy Sunday'

The Equals – 'Baby Come Back'

Canned Heat – 'On the Road Again'

Status Quo – 'Pictures of Matchstick Men'

Stevie Wonder – 'For Once in My Life'

Deep Purple – 'Hush'

Marvin Gaye – 'I Heard it Through the Grapevine'

Amen Corner – 'Bend Me Shape Me / High In the Sky'

The Herd – 'I Don't Want Our Loving to Die'

Bandwagon – 'Breaking Down the Walls of Heartache'

The Showstoppers – 'Ain't Nothin' but A House Party'

The Four Tops – 'Walk Away Renee'

The Foundations – 'Baby Now That I've Found You'

Honeybus – 'I Can't Let Maggie Go'

Judy Collins – 'Both Sides Now'

Diana Ross and the Supremes / The Temptations – 'I'm Gonna Make You Love Me'

I look at these choices from '68 to be the zenith of '60s pop music. So much of it connected with my consciousness and influenced the way I would endeavour to feel about everyday life. Music was a background medium that filled almost every aspect of my waking life, and many of the songs were to resonate with me, especially in the autumn when I started my first meaningful relationship with a girl from the same year group.

Catching trout in Somerset was an angling revelation. It was the first time that I could eat my delicious catch without having to go out to sea! Later that year we would plan a return trip, but with the start of the coarse fishing season, Richard, Frank and I started exploring another tributary of the Thames, the lovely river Kennet.

During the last few weeks of the summer term, I was puzzled by Richard's strange and erratic behaviour. He would be walking around comatose, often unresponsive to any form of questioning and zombie-like in both speech and movement. Eventually I discovered that he was so addicted to his night-time barbel fishing on the River Kennet that he would fish all night, then attend school without any sleep. This went on for about a week, before his inevitable collapse. After a weekend of solid sleeping, he did regain his normal persona.

He also managed to catch some of the elusive large barbel. Neither Frank or I did, though we did have a cracking day's fishing on the same stretch of river with hempseed and maggots.

We employed those same techniques during that summer, fishing with hempseed on the Thames at Wargrave, the Kennet and the Loddon at Twyford. On most occasions we managed to catch huge bags, often 100+ of prime roach and dace, and the bonus of catching pike that were predating on the shoals of silver fish that we had attracted into our swims.

The element of competition was always present. Who would catch the biggest and/or the most?

Tip for Anglers: There is no denying that cooked hempseed is addictive to many species of fish, so today I add a can of commercially prepared hemp to my ground bait, no matter what species I'm after.

Frank proudly displaying his catch from the river Kennet

Our Thames holiday on a punt

Although we had fatally damaged the dinghy, Len Bushnell kindly allowed Frank and I the use of a traditional Thames punt for a week's fishing trip on the Thames. We set off upstream with a massive amount of fishing tackle, bait and camping gear. Instead of punting, we used oars, and inevitably progress upstream against the current was slow. When we were overtaken by a motor cruiser, we would stick our thumbs up to hitch a ride. There is a great comradeship in the boating fraternity, and we were pleasantly surprised by how many tows we received. Our first night was spent fishing the mouth of the River Kennet near Reading. Although we caught some nice chub during the night, the essence of our trip was also the whole camping experience. Bacon and eggs cooked on the Primus stove was a terrific way to start the following morning.

Upstream of Reading, the boat traffic lessoned, and the Thames became narrower and wilder. We would often stop to fish spots that appeared inviting, especially if they could not be accessed by anglers from the bank. Besides the great fishing, the scenery from the perspective of being on the river was stunning. Grand bankside properties with beautiful gardens contrasted with open fields in one vista, followed by steep wooded slopes around the next bend of the river. Instead of Three Men in a Boat, we were Two Young Blokes in a Punt. Frank was determined to make our next overnight stay to be at the Thames-side twin towns of Goring and Streatley.

We moored the punt on the concrete embankment at about 6 p.m. adjacent to the Swan Hotel. As it was late to cook our dinner and being ravenously hungry, the decision to dine at the Swan wasn't difficult. Confusion over the menu meant that we both had a large fish main course, followed by an enormous steak main course, washed down with copious amounts of beer and rum and coke for Frank; draft cider and vodka and lime for me. A very inebriated but happy pair of anglers staggered out of the hotel into torrential rain.

A nearby bridge offered our only shelter, and within minutes we were in our sleeping bags asleep on the hard concrete sloping floor. After about an hour, I awoke to see Frank slowly rolling towards the fast-flowing river. A few more yards and Frank would be taking a midnight dip. His sleeping bag was also tightly knotted around his neck, giving him very little chance of survival should he continue on his route into the Thames. He never really thanked me for shouting and kicking him awake.

Next morning, we reached Abingdon on Thames, where having a swim seemed a refreshing change from fishing. After nearly knocking out the rest of my front teeth by diving into 9 inches of river water, I decided it was safer to stick to catching fish. We were now heading back downstream, and our aim was to stop at some of the alluring fishing spots that we had noticed previously. Progress downstream was rapid and effortless. Night fishing at a remote spot near the Mapledurham estate was spectacular, both of us catching a haul of roach, bream and nuisance eels – despite the noise of what sounded very like a country bumpkin orgy. We decided not to investigate.

Our final night's fishing was above Sonning, one of Richard's favourites spots, as it had the potential to catch big river carp. The venue was a warm water outflow from a coal-fired power station that supplied Reading. All forms of river life thrived there, including fish. During the night the fishing was slow but when Richard joined us at dawn, the fishing became intense. Following some fierce pulls, I was frantically playing the largest carp that we had ever come in contact with. My overriding priority was to safely land the monster fish. Richard and I were perplexed and alarmed when Frank insisted on using his tiny landing net to secure what would have been my largest specimen. Despite telling him to use a larger net, Frank scooped the carp out of the river, only for it to flop back into the Thames, never to be seen again. I was stunned as was Richard. Was this a moment of misjudgement or accidentally on purpose – I shall never know. I guess it was healthy rivalry, though more than half a century later Richard still vividly recalls this tragic incident!

The River Loddon flowed into the Thames just upstream of the boatyard, and on this all-night outing Frank and I had moored the punt across the mouth of the Loddon with the aid of a couple of concrete anchors. The fishing had been really productive until about 1 a.m. As the bites slowed, we both started to doze off into a deep sleep. I was aware of a faint splash close to the punt. This was followed by an ear-piercing scream of such intensity that I assumed I was hearing the sounds of torture, even murder. Instead, it was Frank. A large eel that I had caught earlier had decided to jump out of the keepnet and sliver up Frank's arm, to clamp its teeth onto the collar of his jacket.

After recovering my senses, I pulled the powerful, evil wriggling slime covered eel from his arm and poured us a cup of coffee to calm our nerves. Frank, still trembling, wiped the thick gelatinous slime from his jacket and we both vowed never to keep eels in our nets.

I never did like jellied eel.

A variety of jobs

Besides the landscape gardening job and school cleaner, I tried my hand that summer at being a dustman. Not for me. But there was good money in shovelling out train wagons that were supplying gravel for the construction of the M3 motorway. On one occasion the bucket of the JCB knocked me from the top of the railway truck onto the train tracks of Bracknell railway station. During my fall of about 15 ft, I had time to adjust my leg position to straddle the electrified section. This instinctive reaction prevented a sudden electrifying end – so much for health and safety.

Every time I tried a new job, Engel would offer me more money to return to landscaping. When he offered me £1 per hour, I was happy to weed, lay turf, mow lawns, build patios, etc. for him.

Landscape gardening had an unexpected consequence for me in the summer of 1969, when I was applying for a General Dental Council scholarship. After a glowing reference from the headmaster, I was accepted for an interview at the GDC headquarters on Wimpole St, London. The waiting room was filled with twenty+ candidates, all having achieved at least three grade As at A level and some with S levels. When asked by the other candidates what were my academic achievements, my reply that I had achieved grades of two C's and 1 D won me smiles and glances of encouragement and sympathy. So, not feeling overly optimistic about receiving the extra funding for my 5-year course, should I even be fully accepted at the university of my choice, I decided to treat the interview as a friendly conversation with a few respected gentlemen.

The interview consisted of yours truly versus five professors.

GDC – Halvorsen, why do you want to be a dentist?

Me – I would like to be able to help people and improve their health and well-being.

GDC. *Nods of approval* – When you tell people you are going to be a dentist, what is their reaction?

Me – They say, how can you spend the rest of your life looking into other people's mouths?

GDC – What do you say in response?

Me – I just tell them that I'm resigned to my fate.

GDC – *Howls of laughte*r.

Me, *on a roll* – I spend my holidays working as a landscape gardener, and I believe that dentistry has many similarities.

GDC, *puzzled* – Explain yourself Halvorsen.

Me – Do a good job designing and building a garden, and it will last for years provided it's looked after; I believe the same applies in dentistry.

GDC – *Lots of approving nods.*

The interview lasted for less than 10 minutes and I left having enjoyed the experience.

It would be months before I would know the results of this encounter with the high ups of UK dentistry. I had suggested the money would go on books and study materials such as my very own skull with teeth. If I were to be awarded the scholarship, the allowance would be £1000 per year for 5 years. With the added prospect of being awarded a council educational grant, together with the GDC scholarship, I would be very fortunate.

Back to 1968, after the summer holidays I resumed school knowing this was my last year at Ranelagh. Although the summer's fishing had been fabulous, my love life had been in free fall, but despite experiencing several disastrous breakups, I immediately disobeyed my own dating rules and started seeing a girl from school. The dating started casually but was to turn into my first serious long-term relationship.

By sheer coincidence, Jim of the Honda 50cc fame, started a relationship with a girl who lived near to where I would be spending most evenings at my now steady girlfriend's home. Jim and I would often meet after our dates and compare experiences. Later he would marry his teenage sweetheart and first love.

During schooltime, as my girlfriend Sarah and I were studying different subjects for A level, our time together was scarce. Odd chats over break time were the sum total of our contact during school hours, and being a prefect, I had the use of a prefect's study during rest periods. Most lunch times were filled with either rugby or basketball practice, and the school daytime workload was becoming ridiculously busy.

Due to the fact we had both been busy with studies and me playing sport, I thought it would be good to spend some time with Sarah and asked her if she would like to have a day out with me and my fishing pals. In October Bushnell's held their annual auction of boats at their boat storage yard, adjacent to the backwater. Richard, Frank and I decided to attend, partly out of interest, and partly with the possibility of investing in our own fishing craft – provided the price did not exceed £5. We agreed to divide the cost equally between us. I decided to invite my now steady girlfriend, mainly to give her the impression that we in our own way were affluent forward-thinking investors. Although most of the large, motorised boats would sell for many hundreds of pounds and even these sums would represent knock-down prices, it wasn't until the very last lot – an old wooden skiff 'in need of repair' – that we had the opportunity to bid. After some heart-stopping bidding, we managed to secure it within our price bracket. We celebrated with a drink at the local Greyhound pub in Wargrave.

This was the first time that a girl had attended one of our angling events. Introducing a girl to the lads, I could sense a change in Richard and Frank's attitude towards me. They were sensing that there was a change in the dynamics of our friendships. They were partially correct, as I was spending more time with her and less time fishing or at my home. By Christmas time, I realised that the relationship was becoming increasingly involved and most of my time was being spent at her home and I was being treated like one of the family. Her parents also invited me to landscape their garden, including constructing a large, paved patio area, a lawn and associated flower beds. My first private job.

It was quickly becoming apparent that I was at the beginning of my first 'steady relationship' and my emotional and life priorities were beginning to change. Although most daytime activities including fishing and sports remained reasonably constant, trips to the pub and nightclubs became less frequent. After what appeared to be a short time, even invites to repair our boat and consequent fishing trips diminished. Most of my male friends were becoming distant as I was regarded as being taken.

1968 came to a close with several of my previous 'life goals' significantly altered. Instead of living in the moment and planning my next fishing trip and nights out with the boys, I was starting to think of leaving home, university, life outside the council estate, and the possibility of a long-term romantic relationship. The age of my lack of planning and responsibilities was being substituted by thoughts of a career and possibly settling down.

> 'Now there's more to do than watch my sailboat glide.'
> 'Goin' Back'.

1969

This would be the year of greatest change for me. This was true for most of my friends, both from school and locally. Richard would be studying Dentistry at Birmingham and Frank engineering at a technical college in Rugby.

The year started with the routine of school, homework, various sports, landscaping, dating Sarah and a few memorable fishing trips.

On a mild day in February, I decided to fish on my own at the warm-water outflow just above Sonning on Thames. This was the venue where Frank sabotaged my capture of a large carp and I was hoping for another chance of landing one of these river monsters. Within a few minutes of casting out a lump of bread paste, I was battling a very large fish. Using my trusty 13 ft alloy rod, which was bent double just to hold the fish, I appeared to be making very little impact. After about half an hour, my arms were getting tired, and the fish appeared to be getting stronger and hugging the deep water. Swimming slowly, the leviathan just refused to be beaten, just as I was equally determined not to give up. There was on my part a vague hope that it would eventually tire.

Some young lads who were watching my battle from the iron railings overlooking my swim further drained my confidence when they excitedly and reliably informed me that the carp I was fighting was a monster of at least 20 lb. My fishing tackle was never designed for capturing a fish of this calibre and it became apparent to me that I was the one who was being played! After about another 10 minutes, the outsized carp had decided that enough was enough and headed for a large bed of lilies. As I applied full pressure to stop the fish getting tangled in the weeds, my line snapped. Forty-five minutes of heart stopping and tiring action, and I had nothing but a broken line dangling from my rod top to show for my efforts.

Many will say this is the essence and excitement of angling; and of course, they are correct. On this occasion, however, I kicked my tackle around for a bit, swore a bit, packed up, and went home with the hump.

Over 50 years later, the biggest carp that I have landed still hasn't exceeded 20 lb.

While I was travelling around on my scooter thinking that this was the ultimate in transportation for people of my age group, Richard had passed his driving test and was given a new Bedford van by his parents. This gave him a huge step forward and advantages which us mere motorised two-wheelers could only dream about: the ability to transport massive amounts of fishing tackle and all the accessories across unlimited distances, to travel in comfort and to have a means of staying dry despite the weather.

Following my repeated stories and romancing about the trout fishing in the stream near Nettlecombe Court, we planned a fishing trip during the Easter holidays to the West Country. Our first stop would be the pub in Monksilver, which was only a short distance from our favoured stream. Armed with all our fishing gear, sleeping bags and a Primus stove, we could save on cash for lodgings, leaving more for food and booze.

Heading west on the A303, we made the Notley Arms at Monksilver just before nightfall. We arrived with plenty of time to have a great meal, washed down with the local scrumpy cider – 4 pints for 1s 6d. Sufficiently merry, we managed to negotiate the narrow lanes and settled down close to the small river where we would fish the next morning. We had parked the van in a church graveyard. With the prospect of rain and possibly snow, we decided to sleep in our sleeping bags inside the van.

My abiding memory was waking up to a glass of water that was frozen solid, only inches from our heads. Richard's comment on waking was that we were nearly as stiff and cold as our neighbours underground. The van gave us shelter but very little insulation. Being hungry and cold, I suggested that we walk up to the Field Course Centre and cadge breakfast. Being a similar age as the residents and knowing the buffet set up, we strolled in bold as brass, and helped ourselves to cereal followed by several cups of tea and a full English. Nobody batted an eyelid.

Warmed, fed and watered, we had a wonderful day catching numerous trout by creeping along the stream and 'dapping' worms into likely places. There was a profound sense of achievement from this type of fishing: besides the fun of catching these lovely wild trout, it also assessed our angling skill and knowledge. Sitting on the bank, I was pondering the life and contrast between what my life would have been living in the East End London compared with now. The now was catching edible-sized trout from an enchanted stream in deepest rural Somerset.

As our next stopover was to stay with Richard's aunts, on their farm near Barnstable. We decided to keep the largest fish for our evening meal. Cooked on the Aga, it turned out to be a delicious reward for our efforts.

Richard's two aunts owned a 400-acre farm, much of which borders the Bristol Channel west of Barnstable. Richard and I were given two old double-barrelled 12-gauge shotguns with plenty of cartridges and tasked with shooting any crows, pigeons or rooks that we came across. I had only fired rifles and pistols on a target range, so this was going to be an adventure. We trudged what appeared to be miles across the farmland without seeing any bird life in range of our guns. It was getting near to dusk when we came across a small coppice where a flock of rooks appeared to be settling in for the night. We crept up to the base of the trees and let fire with all barrels, loaded up again and bang, bang, bang, bang. Smoke, the smell of gunpowder and sounds befitting the start of World War Three. Net result: not one dead or injured bird. To add insult to injury, the rooks took off, circled round and landed back on the same trees. It seemed that they were looking down on us with complete disdain: 'Your aim is so bad, why not waste a few more shells on us? We're not worried.'

Richard and I looked at each other and burst out laughing. We both agreed to stick to fishing.

On our return from our West Country trip, the spectre of A Levels loomed. Richard and I were both studying exactly the same subjects but applying for entry into different dental school. Richard had Birmingham as his first choice, whereas I really had only one favourite. I had already sampled the night life in Bristol after a successful entrance interview at the dental hospital. During my interview I admired the principles and ethos of the dentistry syllabus and the way the university was integrated with the city. For me it was Bristol or bust.

Many of my class, including Richard, went into revision hibernation. I did my share of revision, but as was usual for me, I was relying on memory and copious amounts of caffeine to see me through and the taking of written papers. As Bristol dental school had offered me 3 D's as the entry pass levels, I thought this was achievable. I actually achieved 2 C's and 1 D. Today most medical and dental schools require 3 A's. Once I had confirmation of my results, I spent most of the summer in a state of denial. It wasn't until arriving at my Hall of Residence in Clifton Bristol in late September for Fresher's Week, that the full impact and reality hit me: life would never be the same again.

Until I left for university, my priorities were still Sarah, socialising with my estate mates, pubs, nightclubs, and some sport, including the last of the local rugby matches. My steady girlfriend's younger sister was dating a particularly good rugby player called Martin. Like me, Martin was county standard, captaining an undefeated Reading Colts' team. We were both extremely competitive. I captained an undefeated Bracknell Colts' team, and whoever won our crunch match would also win the Berkshire league. To spice up the big deciding match, both sisters came as opposing supporters. As captain, my technical team talk, and tactics consisted of 'Let's beat this bunch of stuck-up snobs.'

It was a great game of rugby, with both sides taking the lead at different moments, everybody playing their A game and players scoring great tries on both sides. With a couple of minutes remaining, Bracknell were down 26 to 28. Being near Reading's try line, I was handed the ball with nobody else to pass to. Nothing for it, but to tuck the ball under my arm and just charge for the line. By sheer determination I scored by carrying four of the opposition's players over the line, either wrapped around my neck or clinging to my waist. As all rugby players know, you must tackle low and hard, which in this case they didn't. Although we, Bracknell won, both teams felt privileged in having taking part in such an enjoyable competitive sporting occasion. Martin and I became friends, even though he would annihilate me every time we played tennis.

By the end of May our exams were over. Our requirement to attend school diminished because there weren't any formal lessons. Teachers started calling us by our first names and most of the conversations revolved around the approaching future. Although this meant more time for fishing and socialising, it was slowly dawning on me that the routine and structure of attending school the lifestyle that I had enjoyed, was coming to an end.

For me, these years of school in the '60s were truly amazing. Saying that, life at university in the early '70s wouldn't be half bad either – but that's another story.

* * *

1969 was another year of incredible music, with extra poignancy for me, as many of the songs I could relate to such as 'Leaving on a Jet Plane' by Peter, Paul and Mary. Soon Sarah and I would be saying our own goodbyes when setting off to our respective universities. As it turned out, the prolonged separations meant that our relationship didn't stand the test of time and we eventually went our separate ways.

> 'I Say a Little Prayer' by Aretha Franklin and 'Angel of the Morning' – Merrilee Rush had an extra poignancy at the time.

Again, my singles list is eclectic:

> The Rolling Stones – 'Honky Tonk Woman'. An all-time disco classic.
>
> The Beatles – 'Get Back', 'Come Together'
>
> Zager & Evans – 'In the Year 2525'. Depressing but Prophetic.
>
> Elvis Presley – 'In the Ghetto'
>
> Jane Birkin & Serge Gainsbourg – '*Je T'aime... mois Non Plus*'. Banned by BBC. Say no more! OK then, one of the most famous *risqué* songs ever recorded.

Creedence Clearwater Revival – 'Proud Mary', 'Bad Moon Rising', 'Green River'

Simon & Garfunkel – 'The Boxer'

The Zombies – 'Time of the Season'

Peter Sarstedt – 'Where Do You Go to My Lovely'

Tom Jones – 'I'll Never Fall in Love Again'

The Temptations – 'I Can't Get Next to You'

Diana Ross & The Supremes & The Temptations – 'I'm Gonna Make You Love Me'

Fleetwood Mac – 'Albatross', 'Man of the World', 'Need Your Love So Bad'

Edwin Starr – 'Twenty-Five Miles,

Marvin Gaye – 'I Heard It Through the Grapevine. People were impressed by my 'snake hips' when dancing to this.

Thunderclap Newman – 'Something in the Air'. A classic atmospheric which brings back the mood of Woodstock and the other music festivals of that year.

The Hollies – 'He Ain't Heavy, He's My Brother'

Jethro Tull – 'Living In the Past'. Ian Anderson's stage persona belies a talented musician and businessman.

David Bowie – 'Space Oddity'

Family Dogg – 'Way of Life'

Humble Pie – 'Natural Born Boogie'

Noel Harrison – 'The Windmills of Your Mind'

Glen Campbell – 'Wichita Lineman'

Mama Cass – 'It's Getting Better'

Smokey Robinson & The Miracles – 'The Tracks of My Tears'. Absolute classic.

Junior Walker & The All Stars – 'Road Runner'. Love it.

The Foundations – 'Build Me Up Buttercup'

Crazy Elephant – 'Gimme Gimme Good Lovin''

Cream – 'Badge'

Led Zeppelin – 'Whole Lotta Love'. Amazing, and led me to buy their first two albums, even though I didn't have a record player at university.

Some of the great albums of 1969 that I enjoyed are:

Let It Bleed – Rolling Stones

Abbey Rd, Yellow Submarine – Beatles

Led Zeppelin 1, Led Zeppelin 11 – Led Zeppelin. Maybe the best rock albums ever recorded.

Tommy – The Who

The Band – The Band

Santana – Santana

On the Threshold of a Dream – Moody Blues

Clouds – Joni Mitchell

To my mind the music of 1969 has become another vintage and shaped much of the early '70s both in new sounds and bands. The reign of the Beatles would be over although their songs and music are timeless. The Rolling Stones, however, are only a fraction of the way through their phenomenal careers. However, for me, their early albums and singles were their best. Much of the '60s music is still played, or covered, or adapted – a testament to the unique development of popular music.

Partly because of my first serious relationship with a girl, and partly due to the dramatic changes to my personal circumstances, I still find that listening to many of the songs of 1969 will vividly conjure the atmosphere, emotions and excitement that I experienced during that amazing year. Even today, a few introductory bars of one of these songs will transport me back to that period.

Long live all '60s music and those in the media who continue to play it. Best wishes to Tony B, still a favourite DJ of mine.

Although I wasn't a great fan, David Bowie's 'Space Oddity' was a very deliberate release linked to the increased activities of manned space missions. For most people, the most significant event of the year was the Apollo 11 moon landing. At the time, anybody with access to a TV was awestruck at the pictures being beamed from the Moon.

Woodstock

The four days of 15–18 August saw the most iconic rock festival of the '60s. Despite a raging global pandemic and being poorly organised, over half a million people gathered to listen to pop and rock music. Compared with today, the media coverage was relatively sparse. Despite lack of publicity, many of the artistes would become icons due to their performances at Woodstock. Participants included Jimi Hendrix, Joan Baez, the Who, Sly and the Family Stone, The Band, Grateful Dead, Creedence Clearwater Revival, Janis Joplin and Ravi Shankar, Crosby Stills and Nash (and Young), Santana and Joe Cocker. There were many lesser knowns such as Tim Hardin, Arlo Guthrie, Canned Heat, Ten Years After and Blood Sweat and Tears. Most of the UK media focused on the mud, nudity, sex and drugs rather than the music. Besides being one of the largest numbers of mega singers and musicians performing at one venue, Woodstock also represented a mass gathering of those believing in the counterculture movement.

As the decade progressed people were able to access music via radio, television, dances, nightclubs and even as background music in shops, etc. The great pop music of the early and mid-60s was constantly being replayed, creating 'database' for the future. Many of the early tracks quickly became classics and were played all through the decade. Even today we are still dancing to many of the songs both upbeat and smoochy. I am sure that '60s music will continue to be played especially at social functions way into the future. Who today wouldn't get up for a jig around on hearing the opening bars of 'Brown Sugar'?

There were three films that were the 1969 standouts for me:

> *Easy Rider*. Starring Peter Fonda, Dennis Hopper and Jack Nicholson. A disturbing 'counterculture' film. For me this film has a fantastic opening music track; 'The Pusher' / 'Born to Be Wild' – Hoyt Axton / Steppenwolf.
>
> *Butch Cassidy and the Sundance Kid* with Paul Newman and Robert Redford. The hit song from the film was 'Raindrops Keep Falling on My Head', BJ Thomas.
>
> *Midnight Cowboy*. With Dustin Hoffman and Jon Voight. Another sad and thought-provoking movie with great music tracks. 'Everybody's Talkin', Harry Nilsson.

Unlike most previous films of the '60s where the cavalry came to the rescue and good triumphs over evil, these films all had tragic endings.

The Green Berets starring John Wayne 1968 was a classic 'war recruitment film'. Later films like *The Deer Hunter* (1978) and *Apocalypse Now* (1979) may have been banned if shown in the '60s for depicting a more realistic and grittier version of the Vietnam war.

Being fascinated by Aliens and UFO's, I found it interesting that Project Blue Book was closed. Started in the '50s this was the USA's official long-standing investigation into aliens and UFOs. The project was terminated not because there wasn't any evidence of aliens, but because they decided that they weren't any threat to national security!

Many events of 1969 would have significant impact for the future.

The lead singer of the Doors, Jim Morrison was tried and convicted of exposing himself before 10,000 people in Miami – changing history? Not really.

The start of the troubles in Northern Ireland (Battle of the Bogside).

Rupert Murdoch takes over *News of the World*.

Yasser Arafat appointed leader of PLO.

Test Flights of Concorde and Boeing 747.

John Lennon and Yoko Ono in 'Bed In' for Peace.

The Cuyahoga River in Cleveland Ohio was so polluted, that it actually caught fire, leading to the Clean Water Act, and the creation of the Environment Protection Agency.

Stonewall Riots in New. York marking the start of the Gay Rights Movement.

Colour TV on BBC1 and ITV.

British 50 pence coin to replace ten bob notes.

Cold War – Strategic Arms Limitation Talks (SALT1) started.

Socially and geopolitically, the rate of change in the world would have a significant impact on the near and distant future.

> 'Let everyone debate the true reality
> I'd rather see the world the way it used to be.'
> 'Goin Back'

Preparing to leave home

Organising everything from accommodation, books and essentially all the requirements for living away from my parents appeared to happen by magic. During the time before starting my new life at Bristol, I decided to focus on the everyday chores and close my mind to the apprehension I was feeling for the direction that my life was to be heading.

Before setting off for the start of Fresher's Week, my daily routine at home remained fairly normal. Lots of conversations with my buddies about our uncertain futures and virtually zero planning of future fishing trips and social activities. Also there seemed to be little point in becoming involved in any local sports activities. I continued the landscape gardening job and the completion of building a patio and landscaping for Sarah's parents. This felt a little strange because she had already left home for her nursing school. It became apparent that classroom friends were planning their post-school futures and that life outside Ranelagh would never be the same again for me.

With a battered suitcase parked next to me, my journey by train to Temple Meads station was pleasantly occupied by chatting to a fellow new dental student called Graham. Although he came from a different social background, we became immediate friends. This made for an encouraging start to my introduction to university life. One of my earliest observations was that I could predict what a student was studying by the length of their hair. Trainee dentists, doctors and vets would in general dressed conservatively and have short tidy hair, whereas the rest, especially the arts students, looked like full-blown hippies.

At my halls of residence, the excitement of meeting new people, living in a city and all that goes with being a student was almost overwhelming. Confirmation that the council was to cover all my university fees and provide a generous grant to live by helped with any financial worries. Together with my scholarship, it meant that I was in a comparatively comfortable financial position. As most shops and venues offered student discounts, I couldn't really regard myself as hard-up.

After a few weeks, I began reflecting on my life in Bracknell. It had been a great twelve years of my formative life. All my friends were also wary of change and for me, although excited for what lay ahead I couldn't help but wonder at times if I had made the right decision.

'Let everyone debate the true reality
I'd rather see the world the way it used to be
A little bit of freedom's all we lack,
So, catch me if you can I'm goin' back'

My first term in Bristol

Having arrived at Bristol Temple Meads railway station, I realised there was no going back. The halls of residence were situated in a beautiful residential part of Bristol called Leigh Woods. My student accommodation was a large room in a grand Victorian building within a stone's throw of the Clifton Suspension Bridge. This most famous landmark spanned the awesome Avon Gorge, and was built by Isambard Kingdom Brunel. Crossing the bridge was to become part of my everyday journey to the university.

My new roommate and future friend Dave had arrived shortly before me. He was a Londoner with a broad Cockney accent. He was studying something like Politics and Economics. We immediately hit it off and having both arrived a week before the start of term, our immediate discussion was how to enjoy Fresher's Week.

A visit to the Student's Union to view the social events, clubs and associations that the university had on offer and potentially join, was to be a must for Dave and me. Joining the Medics rugby club, the university basketball team and the debating society appeared to be a good start. Besides the cheap drinks and food, we found ourselves immersed in invitations to parties and clubs along with hundreds of students of a similar age and outlook, all seeking the same social opportunities. So far, the initial impression of student life in Bristol was looking promising. Initially there appeared to be almost too many opportunities to choose from, and I was potentially heading into an early burnout.

The bridge

It was Sunday in mid-December, and I had decided to spend the weekend in my halls of residence on my own. Perhaps it was too much partying together with too much drink the night before, but I found myself missing my friends new and old, my family and home life in general. I was feeling down, really negative and for the first time in my life depressed. While I was trying to catch up on some homework, my radio was playing a series of sad and relevant songs which reflected my perceived situation. Peter, Paul and Mary's version of 'Leaving on a Jet Plane', Fleetwood Mac's 'Man of the World', Marmalade's 'Reflections of My Life', and Dusty Springfield's 'Goin' Back' were some of my downers. The final straw came when 'Reflections' was played again, and I started sobbing uncontrollably. Until this moment, I had never considered myself to be a negative person devoid of positive emotions.

One hundred yards from my room, I found myself standing in the middle of the Clifton Suspension bridge looking down the 200-foot drop into the muddy waters of the River Avon.

There was no fear, but a solution to end my acute emotional pain was to jump.

Could I have jumped? Yes.

Did I? No.

What stopped me was my innate curiosity for the future and what I would be missing, even if the pain and despair were to continue.

Wow. I am so grateful and thankful that a momentary decision of mine was challenged and reversed. I believe that something in the universe pulled me back, and my sense of self-preservation kicked in. Looking back at that situation, I was fortunate; many young students' lives have been lost under similar circumstances.

It was also an example of how deeply I could be affected by music.

> 'All my sorrow
> Sad tomorrow
> Take me back to my old home
> All my crying [all my crying]
> Feel I'm dying, dying
> Take me back to my old home
> I'm changing, arranging
> I'm changing, I'm changing everything
> Ah, everything around me
> The world is a bad place
> A bad place, a terrible place to live
> Oh, but I don't wanna die'
>
> 'Reflections of My Life', Marmalade

For the past 30 plus years I have been involved in the pursuit of happiness, longevity and healthy ageing. Since that time on the bridge, although life has sometimes had its ups and downs, not a moment has gone by when departing this world has been an option. If I had made the wrong choice, I would not have had fifty years in a loving and happy marriage, two wonderful sons and nine beautiful grandchildren.

The Mandrake

During Freshers Week I could not resist the opportunity to visit a nightclub. A disco evening had been advertised for students at a private member's club, the Mandrake. This was the very same club that Guy, the sales manager who had given me a lift in this TR5, had recommended. The Mandrake was *the* nightclub in Bristol to have a membership. Sited in a quiet side street near the offices of the world-famous Harveys Bristol Cream, the club was also conveniently close to the city centre.

It was made up of a series of dimly lit interconnected storage caves, I was immediately captivated by the sophisticated atmosphere. The club didn't open until 9 p.m. and there was always a long queue of hopefuls trying to gain admission. As luck would have it, on my first visit I was warmly greeted by Guy. He was good friends with the club's owners, John and Barbara. After Guy had made the introductions, I became a member within an hour and was also offered the position of part-time disc jockey. My passion for the type of music that was appropriate for dances, discos and nightclubs had helped create this brilliant opportunity. Now I was able to combine my love of being part of the disco/nightclub scene with all the associated social life, and to be paid for it!

John had given up his career as manager in a Woolworths store to start the nightclub. His strategy was to invite 'high rollers', especially if they owned a flash car which could then be displayed in a nearby car park. This would attract the good-looking ambitious girls, who then attracted the wannabe guys. Membership and admission fees, bar and food takings were a formula that seemed to be a recipe for success, and I regarded being associated with the Mandrake club throughout my five years living in Bristol as a 'best of both worlds' lifestyle. It gave me another enjoyable dimension to my student life. Besides supplementing my income as a student, and a source of free drinks and food when working, it expanded my social life. Socialising via the club with city people gave me the opportunity to make friends of both sexes, many of whom were similar in attitude and outlook to my non-student friends left behind in Bracknell.

Many years later, after a twenty-fifth reunion of my fellow Bristol graduates, I decided to buy a shirt in a fashionable shop on Park Street. On entering, I was greeted by a vaguely familiar face. 'Hello, Den, (he remembered I was a dentist!), haven't seen you down the Mandrake lately,' he said in the broadest Bristolian accent. Having been absent for at least 25 years, I just smiled and said that I've been busy and asked him how he was. 'Terrible trouble with me hernial and I's got bad diarrheal.' He then refused to accept any money for the shirt and looked forward to seeing me at the club.

Working on the record turntables was thirsty work and I felt that it was important to gauge the mood of those on the dance floor. My drink of choice was Bacardi and coke – just enough to be fully in tune with the mood of my dancing audience. Although walking back to my flat at 2.30 a.m. meant passing through some trouble spots, I never encountered any violence or threatening behaviour.

Unlike many modern universities, Bristol hasn't a clearly defined campus. Many of the departments were in grand historic buildings, scattered around Clifton and the centre of the city. Many of our lectures and demonstrations were widely integrated within the Bristol Royal Infirmary (BRI) complex.

Very quickly, I made friends with many of my fellow year dental students. Bristol dental school was one of the few universities to accept students from Norway. My surname of Halvorsen meant the Norwegian intake assumed I was one of their compatriots. Within no time we were drinking and discussing all things Scandinavian. Two of these good-looking Norwegian blokes being far from their homeland felt their situation gave them an excuse for a stream of riotous parties and unbecoming behaviour. Frankly it was difficult to keep up with them.

I decided to rekindle my love of rugby and joined the Bristol medics rugby club, which consisted of an amalgamation of student medics, vets and dentists, my social circle was growing beyond my wildest dreams. Although our rugby club could barely muster two teams, the overall standard was very high. Being close to the Welsh border, the 1st team consisted of a disproportionate number of Welshmen. This raised the standard of the rugby for our team, who in turn had to learn all the verses of 'Bread of Heaven' and other Welsh rugby favourites.

After about twenty years without contact, I recently met with a friend and colleague who had shared a rented house with myself while we were students. The talk turned to the subject of cars. As dental students in the same year group, we had an immediate common interest in anything that was motorised and on wheels, especially if it was fast and convertible. My mode of transport was my trusty Lambretta, but it rapidly came to my notice that Frank was driving around Bristol in a vastly superior white Triumph Spitfire. Whenever we spoke, the conversation would return to what mode of transport would replace my scooter once I had passed my driving test. We spent more time looking through motoring magazines for potential cars than on class work. He was, and still is, a mine of information when motorised wheels are concerned. Before long, I decided that my requirements consisted of a vehicle with at least two seats and a weatherproof cover.

Not knowing when I would have a full driving license, my choices were limited. Frank came up with the great idea of the unique 3-wheeler Morgan. We managed to find one advertised for £125 north of Birmingham, and within a few days, I was staring at a 1939, 3-wheel Morgan powered by a Ford 10 engine. I had never driven a car before, let alone a vehicle without reverse or synchromesh gears – without reverse, it could be driven on a motorcycle license. After an eight-hour drive from the Midlands, I arrived home to Bracknell, capable of driving anything, no matter how many wheels.

I was now the proud owner of a rare piece of motoring history. At the time, my only interest was to have the nearest thing to a car, be it a rather peculiar and quirky specimen. By today's standards, it was a 3-wheeled death trap. At speeds of over 70 mph, the stability and steering became non-existent. However, it was great fun and a talking point whenever I used it. On one occasion I was asked if my Morgan could be used for a fellow student's wedding car. It was the only time that I became an unpaid chauffeur, in exchange for an invitation to a wedding of a couple who were complete strangers.

Back at my halls of residence, I was summoned to see the Bursar for disobeying the order to not park the Morgan in an allocated space reserved for motorcycles. My argument that I was driving the Morgan on a motorbike license, and it was classified as a motorcycle didn't seem to cut much ice. We agreed to disagree.

Very shortly afterwards, Dave and I were in front of the Bursar again on a completely different matter. Parked against a wall in our room was a full-size sail, which we had commandeered from a loft. The sail, which we had opened across one wall of our bedroom, wasn't the problem; it was the limericks that all our visitors were requested to scribble on the canvas. Admittedly many were close to the mark, but the torrent of abuse we were subjected to by the Bursar was stunning. Admittedly he was an English scholar, but the depth of his vocabulary was epic. We didn't realise there were so many denigrating words beginning with D – disgusting, delinquent, dastardly, disgraceful, demented, dirty, despicable, deplorable, depraved, deranged, etc. After this bawling out, Dave and I decided to look for alternative accommodation once our agreed time in halls had expired.

The tiger

On one occasion, a friend and I decided to go to the famous Bristol Zoo. We came across the cage containing the rare white tiger, who was spending time looking at us with a fixed stare, just as we were looking at this impressive beast. Showing off, I started making growling noises and facial expressions to the tiger, expecting a similar retort. This dignified rare animal turned away from us, lifted its tail, and peed onto my face from a distance of at least 6 ft. My incredulity was not about being urinated on; it was the incredible accuracy of the jet stream.

My first few months in Bristol were so eventful that not only was it difficult to take it all in, but the reason for being there – i.e., my studies – was at times secondary to all the new and exciting experiences that were engrossing me. I still had trepidation about where all this massive change from my previous life would take me, and in quiet moments found myself thinking, *Stop the world, I want to get off.*

> 'Now there's more to do than watch my sailboat glide
> And every day can be my magic carpet ride.'
> 'Goin' Back'

By the end of my first term however, I was settling in to the routine of being a student and also concentrating on my studies. The transition between school and university was becoming easier and I was adapting to the new and exciting chapter of my life.

Following a very enjoyable Christmas party at the dental hospital, the next day I returned to Bracknell for the Christmas holidays. Although the last few months had been the most eventful that I had ever experienced, catching up with the gang from the estate was wonderful. Lots of trips to the pub, constant updates, swopping new stories and plenty of reminiscing took place. The constant socialising created a superb seasonal homecoming. However, we all realised that this time was temporary and for most of us 'home' would never be the quite same again.

New Year's Eve, the end of the decade, was for me a fantastic and memorable night, one that capped a phenomenal 10 years. At a party at the Pantiles night club my friends and I celebrated the end of an amazing year, the joys of camaraderie and friendship, and welcomed in the new decade with anticipation and the promise of new beginnings.

EPILOGUE

Although I have now entered my somewhat senior years, I have kept an incredible fondness in my heart for the 1960s. This was an amazing era to grow up in and to be a part of. Writing this book, I have had a chance to relive many of my memories from that time, and who can really forget their formative years? For me, the '60s represented a voyage of discovery; it was a divisive time in world history but also a decade steeped in inspired change for a young boy growing up.

With a tight knit group of friends, a huge passion for fishing and the burgeoning music scene, I embraced the era with the freedom of youth. Many years later, I still believe the '60s and all the excitement of those times lives on in me.

My story here takes me as far as my arrival at Bristol University and where I found myself on the threshold of a new life and a holistic career in dentistry that would span nearly 50 years.

My growing up years were, for the most part, idyllic but little could I have known that the good friends I made back then would still be a big part of my life today, and that Richard, Frank and I still fish and share good times on those same riverbanks. Now our modes of transport are more reliable, our fishing gear more sophisticated, and our stories ever taller, but our fishing techniques remain almost the same. However, I have recently ditched my trusty transistor radio in favour of a Smartphone with a '60s playlist.

Over the years I have taught my sons, nephews and grandchildren the skills of angling and helped create several new generations of fishermen.

During my time at Bristol, I met the love of my life, my wife and best friend Lyn who was studying nursing. Together we raised two wonderful boys and now are proud grandparents to nine amazing grandchildren. I realise the love of family and good friends is irreplaceable. The life we have together is complete in so many ways.

* * *

'Govern a nation as you would cook a small fish. Do not overdo it.'

Lao Tzu

'There is nothing – absolutely nothing – half as much worth doing as simply messing about in boats.'

Kenneth Grahame, *The Wind in the Willows*

'If all politicians fished, instead of spoke publicly, we would be at peace with the world.'

Will Rogers

Give my playlist a listen: Goinbacktothesixties

https://open.spotify.com/playlist/4qCkbNywzqg6h6L95KXNp9?si=F1FjAdg4RYeQz6mohNSnBw&dd=1

Ingram Content Group UK Ltd.
Milton Keynes UK
UKHW021431220623
423881UK00032B/416